Contents

Foreword

Our first response to the NHS reforms, published in November 1990, described them as a move from ration-book collectivism to market socialism. And the study, *The NHS Reforms: Whatever Happened to Consumer Choice?*, argued that the NHS would remain 'a producer-dominated monopoly which ekes out service to patients at the discretion of the authorities'. After four years of experience, should we in all fairness revise our judgment?

It must be conceded that GP fundholding has yielded more benefits than seemed likely at the outset, and it should be acknowledged that some hospital trusts have tried hard to improve their responsiveness to consumers. However, from an economic standpoint the NHS reforms do not represent much of an advance. The power of the medical and political authorities over consumers is as entrenched as ever; and continued reliance on taxation for finance means that rationing is endemic. Treatments are, in some cases, withheld, and in others provided only after long and clinically unjustified delays. The reasons why the consumers' interests cry out for an alternative method of financing health care are described in a succinct but insightful essay by Arthur Seldon, once the IEA's Editorial Director and still its intellectual inspiration.

But the main purpose of this collection is to gauge the reactions of the medical profession to the reforms, now that a decent interval has elapsed. As the contributors reveal with great clarity in their own words, the reformed NHS still leaves a lot to be desired.

The idea of producing a collection of essays representing a cross-section of medical opinion was suggested by Sir Reginald Murley and it has been his energy that carried the project through to completion, thus providing me with the perfect opportunity to thank him for his loyal and hard-working efforts as a member of the Advisory Council since the inception of the Health and Welfare Unit in 1986.

Dr David G. Green

The IEA Health and Welfare Unit

Choice in Welfare No. 23

Patients or Customers:
Are the NHS Reforms Working?

Sir Reginald Murley (Editor)

J.I.L. Bayley
Gillian and Ben FitzGerald
Geoffrey Glazer
Robert Kennedy
Hamish Laing
John C. Nicholls

Commentaries by

Peter Collison
Arthur Seldon
Sir Richard Storey

IEA Health and Welfare Unit
London, 1995

First published June 1995

The IEA Health and Welfare Unit
2 Lord North St
London SW1P 3LB

© The IEA Health and Welfare Unit 1995

ISBN 0-255 36360-5

Typeset by the IEA Health and Welfare Unit
in New Century Schoolbook 10 on 11 point
Printed in Great Britain by
St Edmundsbury Press Ltd
Blenheim Industrial Park, Newmarket Rd
Bury St Edmunds, Suffolk

The Authors

J.I.L. Bayley is Consultant Orthopaedic Surgeon at the Royal National Orthopaedic Hospital in Stanmore.

Peter Collison was born in London and went to Birmingham University and then to Nuffield College, Oxford. He remained in Oxford as a Lecturer in Sociology until 1965 when he became Professor of Social Studies at the University of Newcastle upon Tyne. He has published widely in professional journals particularly in the field of urban sociology, and has been at various times Rockefeller Fellow at the University of Chicago and Chairman of the Social Affairs Committee of the Economic and Social Research Council. For sixteen years he served on the South Tyneside Health Authority and subsequently served this Authority's successor as Adviser to its Community Unit.

Ben and **Gillian FitzGerald** are members of a six partner practice in the semi-rural green belt area of Radlett. Ben FitzGerald qualified at The Middlesex Hospital and worked for several years in hospital medicine, gaining his MRCP at The Royal Free. He has no regrets about leaving hospital medicine for the microcosm of general practice.

His wife, Gillian, qualified at Cambridge University and was first into general practice, initially in Islington in North London. The differences in general practice in the Inner City and in Radlett are many and varied.

Geoffrey Glazer, MS FRCS FACS is Senior Consultant Surgeon at St Mary's Hospital, London. Mr Glazer trained at St Mary's Hospital and in the United States where he was Research Fellow at Harvard Medical School. Mr Glazer is an Examiner at the Royal College of Surgeons of England and is Past President of the Pancreatic Society of Great Britain and Ireland.

Mr Glazer has been Clinical Director of Surgery and Chairman of the Division of Surgery at St Mary's Hospital. He is Director of a large surgical training programme and sits on various working groups at the Royal College of Surgeons of England and the Association of Surgeons of Great Britain and Ireland.

Robert Kennedy is the senior partner of a town practice in West Hertfordshire. The practice has approximately 15,000 patients served by seven doctors. He has been a principal in primary care for over 30 years and, on reflection, would not have wanted to spend his time otherwise. The practice is patient-centred and he has been the lead partner in fundholding affairs since the practice joined the first wave of fundholders, but sees himself more as a member of a team than necessarily its director.

Hamish Laing is a Senior Registrar in Plastic Surgery in Wales. Previously he worked at Mount Vernon Hospital in Northwood, Middlesex. A first-wave trust, this is the regional centre for burns, plastic and reconstructive surgery for North Thames (West) providing an outpatient, day surgery and emergency service to many other hospitals in the region. A recent merger with Watford district general hospital has seen the Mount Vernon Trust dissolved and a new two-site trust formed.

Sir Reginald Murley graduated in medicine in 1939, then served in the RAMC for six and a half years, initially in field units and then as a trainee and surgical specialist in orthopaedic, plastic and general surgery. After World War II he was engaged in teaching and research at Barts before appointment as consultant surgeon in the NHS at St Albans and the Royal Northern and, later, honorary consultant surgeon to Barts. He has contributed numerous articles to the medical literature on a wide variety of subjects and is the author or co-author of a number of surgical and related books. He has served as a surgical tutor, regional adviser, examiner and then member of Council of the Royal College of Surgeons of England, culminating in his presidency from 1977-80, and then chairmanship of the Hunterian Trustees since 1988. He has also been president of four other medical societies.

John C. Nicholls is a Consultant General Surgeon in both NHS and private practice, but has been interested in health service management since his return from working overseas for five years in 1979. Initially he served on the District Management Team, then Board of the North West Hertfordshire Health Authority, but is now the Medical Director of the St Albans and Hemel Hempstead NHS Trust which came into being in 1994.

Arthur Seldon is a Founder President of the IEA and Founder Editor of *Economic Affairs*. His main publications include *Pensions in a Free Society*, IEA, 1957; *The Great Pensions Swindle*, Tom Stacey, 1970; *Capitalism*, Blackwell, 1990; *The State Is Rolling Back*, E. & L. Books and IEA, 1994. As a result of his longstanding interest in the economics of health care, including studies of the NHS in Britain as well as systems in Israel, Australia and the USA, Arthur Seldon wrote *After the NHS*, IEA, 1968; and drafted *Health Service Financing*, the Report of a British Medical Association committee, in 1970. He was one of two 'patients' (the other a later Chancellor of the Exchequer) on the committee with 10 medical professionals, and he concluded that the NHS would have to be reformed both internally, to incorporate market disciplines, and exposed to competition from private medicine in the external market.

Sir Richard Storey has been Chairman of Portsmouth & Sunderland Newspapers plc since 1973. He was Chairman of the Press Association Limited, is a past President of the Newspaper Society and a member of the European Newspaper Publishers' Association (ENPA). He is a director of The Fleming Enterprise Investment Trust plc, Foreign & Colonial Smaller Companies plc. He is Chairman of The Sir Harold Hillier Gardens and Arboretum Management Committee; a Trustee of the Foundation and Friends of the Royal Botanic Gardens, Kew; Chairman of York Health Services Trust; and was High Sheriff for North Yorkshire, 1992/93.

Editor's Introduction

Sir Reginald Murley

Ever since the start of the National Health Service I have felt that patients, doctors and other health workers needed a much better appreciation of the economic facts of life. But how could this ever become possible in a state near-monopoly and with a virtually free-at-the-time service?

In 1976, just a year before I became President of the Royal College of Surgeons of England, I submitted evidence to the Royal Commission on the National Health Service, based upon my then 28 years experience of both NHS and private practice, stressing the virtues of symbiosis between them. Moreover I pointed out that the sensible encouragement of a thriving independent sector, alongside a more enlightened and consumer-sensitive NHS, might modestly promote Aneurin Bevan's belief that 'in an ideal world we would all be private patients'.

Many years ago I suggested that, for the better enlightenment of the patient, the price of all pharmaceuticals and dressings should be printed on the container or wrapping. Consumers would thus become aware of some of the costs of their care, even though many might be entitled to substantial rebates or to entirely free-at-the-time drugs. The possibility that the price of some drugs might even then be less than the fairly modest early prescription charge was also foreseen. Indeed, nowadays it is not uncommon for the prescription charge to exceed the overall cost of many medicines—a matter of which the patient should surely be made aware.

Billing the Patient

But, in my 1976 evidence, I also advocated a minimum first step in hospital cost-accounting by suggesting that every in-patient should be given a fairly simple bill for the services received. On one side of that bill the overall cost of care would be shown, based upon the *average* daily charge. After recording the total cost there would be appended a small lodging charge and the difference between the two would be recorded as the final 'Charge to the Exchequer'. A footnote would also explain how an Exchequer contribution of, say, £1,180 was made up from a national insurance contribution of £118 with the remaining £1,062 provided from general taxation. On the reverse of such a bill (rather in the style of the former local rate demand with which many people were already familiar) would be a more detailed breakdown of hospital costs—salaries, wages, pharmaceuticals, operation room charges, etc. Thus, without attempting to give a detailed account of the costs for each individual patient's care, all would become better aware of the economic facts of life.

It was also my belief that, for the better information of the doctors in charge of each hospital patient, a copy of the bill should be appended to the front sheet of the hospital notes, thus being readily available when case summaries were prepared. Moreover, during my later years in private practice, it was my routine to include a copy of each patient's hospital account with my medical notes. I found it especially helpful and informative to be given this opportunity to learn precisely what every patient (or his/her insurer) had paid the hospital, thus giving each of us a better appreciation of our crucial interdependence. But more and more I began to ask why this was not feasible in the NHS.

Pseudo-Markets

Although, with my father having become a naturalised American subject, I had some knowledge of Medicare, Medicaid, Diagnosis Related Groups, Health Maintenance and Preferred Provider Organisations in the USA, I must confess that I little suspected that we would ever introduce a purchaser/provider system in this country. In addressing a meeting on British and American Health Care Systems in January 1987 I said: 'For some years past I have advocated the creation of a "pseudo-market" within our NHS (which) could be achieved by credit transfer of funds between health authorities.' What I had in mind was that the funding of hospital care should be provided by the health district in which the patient lived and then transferred to the hospital providing specialist care. A successful specialist unit or individual doctor would tend to attract patients from a wider area than the immediate neighbourhood: this would reward those who actually did the work rather than allocating funds on a rigid bureaucratic basis. The beauty of such a system, in the absence of private item-of-service or of a funded government insurance scheme, would be that centres attracting large numbers of patients would receive commensurately better funding, whereas others would receive less.

Above all, the sort of 'pseudo-market' which I suggested could ensure that the money followed the patient. I also envisaged that most patients might make some personal contribution to the costs of their care and that many would actively participate in decision-making about the most appropriate provider. Without such positive collaboration between patients, doctors and other providers (whether government or privately funded) we cannot begin to ensure that our overall medical and economic resources are more appropriately and efficiently used. Above all, the ultimate decisions about marrying up unlimited demand with available resources would be shared between doctors and patients, as well as the various providers and purchasers.

The purchaser/provider system now operating in our own NHS was introduced by the present government in 1990. It has been in operation long enough for those at the sharp end of the equation—the doctors and their patients—to attempt to give a reasonably fair assessment of its strengths and weaknesses. And so the advisory council of the IEA Health and Welfare Unit decided that the time had come to invite some of those doctors, working so-to-speak 'at the coalface', to tell us of their experience. The authors of the five main essays included in this book, have been scrupulously selected. They are all hardworking doctors who can be depended upon to give a reasonably fair and objective description of their present situation. Each of them was invited to give an honest and considered account of the way in which the new budgeting system affected them and especially their patients. I have studied these contributions with great interest. They do not tell one simple story, but they clearly circumscribe the problems and some of the advantages which may have accrued from these changes.

What is most apparent from these essays, even those which paint a more favourable picture, is that the patient is plainly following the money rather than the money following the patient. I think that I can best illustrate this last point by saying that, however good and efficient my own family doctor might be, I would most emphatically not give him financial control of my own, and my wife's, private insurance funds. Therefore, why should I give my doctor, or some more distant medical or lay bureaucrat, control of the health revenue I have provided by taxation?

Patient Power

If the funds really did follow the patient, and if the patient were empowered to play a more active part in the decision-making process by being allowed to shop around and, if necessary, to make supplementary payments to a possibly more costly doctor or hospital which he regarded as superior, the consumer would clearly be in an entirely different ball-game. Notwithstanding the assertion of some budgeting doctors (e.g. Robert Kennedy) that they have been able to improve their in-house services, I remain doubtful as to whether their patients are always getting a better and more sensitive hospital service. It is apparent that some of those patients, by virtue of providing cash-starved hospitals with much needed finance, are often jumping queues in disregard of acceptable personal and clinical priority. Furthermore, as Hamish Laing shows, a patient may have to change hospitals more than once to secure a first outpatient appointment simply because the purchaser has switched the budget to another provider.

Although these papers were primarily commissioned to provide an overview of the purchaser/provider system, some of the authors, and Geoffrey Glazer in particular, have highlighted a number of related changes in the hospital service which have exacerbated many of the problems of budgeting and certainly done little to mitigate them. Glazer rightly states that clinical costing is still in its infancy; that there is a growing risk of hospitals and outpatients being run like the wrong sort of conveyor-belt factory; that patients can arrive in the middle of the night before major surgery, and that their rapid discharge results in greater pressure on GPs as well as the need for some to be re-admitted with complications. Moreover, there are often special difficulties resulting from the sometimes excessive growth of day surgery.

Despite several approaches to busy physicians we were unable to persuade anyone to give an account of hospital budgeting in the general or specialist medical service. This may partly be explained by the relatively small number of medical patients now admitted for investigation, which was common in the past, and by the high proportion of beds occupied by medical emergencies which are not subject to purchaser/provider contracting. But the costing of medical outpatient consultations and related investigations does not materially differ from that on the surgical side, being based upon average costing for the various specialist medical clinics.

Prior to these reforms a patient could be referred to virtually any NHS consultant, specialist unit or hospital, of his and his doctor's choice, without let or hindrance. That was certainly true of the NHS when I worked in it between 1948 and 1980. Moreover, for many years I did not have a conventional waiting list, but admitted most patients for elective surgery on a firm date. We were also able to give a prompt outpatient appointment to every woman with a breast lump, and admission within the succeeding week for those requiring an operation. If the present system, which certainly makes purchasers and providers better aware of the financial facts of life, can be reformed so as to restore that degree of flexibility and freedom for the patient, I would be prepared to give it my support. But I would also need to be convinced that the additional costs and needs of the undergraduate and postgraduate teaching hospitals, and of many specialist centres of excellence and research, were properly covered as well. I just wonder what Adam Smith would have thought about all this? I rather fancy that he would have favoured the health voucher as one method of better empowering the consumer. I also suspect that he would have favoured a genuine health insurance fund freed, so far as possible, from political interference. Notwithstanding my more sceptical comments, I warmly commend these papers for careful study by all who are seriously concerned about the present and future state of the National Health Service.

'The Patient's Needs will always be Paramount'

A Provider's View

Hamish Laing

In 1993/4 Hamish Laing worked in the sub-regional plastic surgery department at University College Hospital, London (now University College London Hospitals). As a small unit it was vulnerable to the pressures of the reforms, the Tomlinson report and the reduction in capitation of its local purchasers. During his year there University College Hospital was closed with patients being smuggled across picket lines by managers. The plastic surgery unit moved to a smaller ward in The Middlesex Hospital. A major reduction in work-force and services ensued and junior managerial posts were in constant flux.

Hamish Laing's interest in 'the reforms' grew from this chaos. In order to provide a service and acquire a training, he became involved in the day-to-day organisation of the unit, negotiating with purchasers about extra-contractual referrals and developing structured prices to better reflect resource utilisation. His paper is a personal view of the purchaser/provider split and, although anonomised, all examples concern real patients.

The most recent reforms of the National Health Service (NHS), and in particular the division of health care provision into 'providers' and 'purchasers', represents the greatest change in the organisation of NHS funding and health planning since its inception. Although the changes covered primary, secondary and tertiary care, this paper will concentrate on their effects on the acute hospital service.

With regard to hospitals the reforms were intended to:

☐ Distinguish between the *provision* of health care and the *purchase* of it: a role previously shared by the District Health Authority (DHA) and thus 'to make the Health Service more responsive to the needs of patients...'[1]

☐ Allow greater choice for patients and their General Practitioners (GPs) by enabling 'hospitals which best meet the needs and wishes of patients to get the money to do so, the money required to treat patients will be able to cross administrative boundaries'.[2] That is to say that *'the money would follow the patient'*.

☐ Encourage hospitals to be more flexible in planning provision responsive to perceived local need by devolving responsibility to local managers from the Regions and DHA's, and to develop patient orientated services. These might include giving appointment times that are realistic, providing outreach clinics in GP's surgeries or extending the availability of multi-disciplinary clinics, such as skin cancer clinics with plastic surgeons and dermatologists working alongside each other.

It was implicit in the White Paper that considerable economy could be achieved easily within the NHS. In her foreword Prime Minister Margaret Thatcher said:

Taken together, the proposals represent the most far-reaching reform of the National Health Service in its forty year history ... We believe that a National Health Service that is run better, will be a National Health Service that can care better. ... The patient's needs will always be paramount.[3]

At the inception of the changes in April 1991 considerable concern was expressed that the new system of funding secondary health care with a substantial increase in administrative costs would drain resources from patient care and lead to under-provision of services. Ministers were quick to reassure the public that, if the reforms identified a real lack of resources in the system, additional funds would be forthcoming. It was recognised that some hospitals (providers) might not prove to be viable financially if subjected to market forces. Ministers would need to take unpopular decisions, particularly in the major cities. London was singled out as having too many acute hospital beds to the detriment of primary care. Some Ministers clearly felt that the close proximity of the private sector had a deleterious effect on the running of some NHS departments in central London.

Fundamental to the reforms was the establishment of NHS hospital trusts (trusts) and fundholding GP practices (GPFH). In the first year few hospitals became trusts and GPFHs remained in the minority so that the true 'market' did not operate until 1993/4. Even now the special health authorities (SHAs) remain 'protected' until 1994/5.

In 1991/2 many absurdities arose as the fledgling found its feet, but it is perhaps unfair to judge the reforms on that basis—although the patients adversely affected have done so. It is the performance of the system that is now in place that should be assessed against the grand vision expressed in *Working for Patients* six years ago. Nearly all acute providers are trusts, some having already been swallowed up in mergers. Regional health authorities (RHAs) have been reduced further in number and importance. Purchasing authorities have settled into their new strategic role, some in partnership with the family health service authorities (FHSAs). Although less popular than predicted, many more GPs are either fundholding or purchasing services in consortia. How then have the reforms matched up to their objectives, and have the patient's needs remained paramount?

Plastic and Reconstructive Surgery in London

Before those questions can be answered it is necessary to consider the situation of plastic surgery in Greater London. The specialty is relatively small amongst hospital services and is predominantly based in large regional (as they were) centres around the periphery of Greater London where they have a high profile amongst both the local and more distant population that they serve. They are supported in this task by smaller sub-regional units based predominantly in the teaching hospitals, each with formal links to a regional unit. Sub-regional units have relatively few beds and consultant sessions compared to other acute specialties and are thus vulnerable to pressure from within their hospital if funding is scarce.

Plastic and reconstructive surgery is poorly understood by the public, purchasers and some colleagues in respect of the scope of work performed and the role played in collaborating with many other specialists: e.g. soft tissue cover of the compound orthopaedic injury, the repair of pressure sores in the neuropathic patient, the closure of sternal defects following cardiac surgery and, topically, achieving skin cover in patients with necrotising fasciitis. One London purchaser, whose knowledge of plastic surgery seemed to come from glossy magazines, refused to accept that 30 per cent of the unit's activity was emergency surgery, and insisted on inspecting the operating theatre registers before they would settle the contract. They had not appreciated the volume of hand and soft-tissue trauma that their residents suffer.

Some purchasers seeking to ration hospital care provision have produced 'low priority' lists of procedures which they will not routinely fund, and many of these fall within the remit of plastic surgery. Indeed in 1992/3 one purchaser did not place a single block contract for elective plastic surgery. Yet many of their proscribed procedures yield higher Quality-Adjusted Life Years (QUALYs)[4] and cost-benefit than the treatments considered acceptable.[5]

Plastic surgery has been exposed in London to the harsh realities of the market to a greater extent than some other specialties, as purchasers seek to achieve substantial savings in their hospital contracts to match falling capitation revenue and to allow a shift in emphasis towards primary and community services. In addition the regional units have been able to sub-specialise their consultants' interests in such a way as to attract patients from across the country. One regional unit had patients on its waiting list from 128 purchasers of which only 14 had a contract with the hospital. Such a unit is vulnerable to under-funding within the Extra-contractual Referral (ECR) process.

Have the Reforms Succeeded in their Objectives?

□ To Split the Purchaser from the Provider

This has clearly been achieved now that nearly all provider hospitals are trusts. The interim phase of Directly Managed Units (DMU's) was unsatisfactory and allowed first-wave trusts to gain a competitive advantage. In addition some early trusts benefited from capital investment in, for example, information technology and resource management which was not available to later trust applicants. However the take up of fundholding has been much more patchy. There are very few GPFH practices in central London for example, where many practices have insufficient patients to qualify and those that do are not enthusiastic about the potential benefits.

In fact most (but not all) procedures undertaken by plastic surgeons are excluded from GPFH purchasing, being invoiced instead to the DHA. Outpatient referrals, however, are not excluded. Plastic surgery has therefore been unable to benefit from the purchaser power of GPFH's who may find that their patients can be seen for an outpatient opinion, but that the procedure is then blocked by the DHA.

It has become clear that, to survive, a provider must have a firm grip on the collection of data. One centre, a first-wave trust, achieves 99 per cent coding and invoicing within six weeks of a patient's discharge and 'misses' less than 10 ECRs a year. Another unit has a 75 per cent coding rate and misses 10 ECRs a month. As contracts become more sophisticated (banded prices, cost and volume etc.) so the penalties for poor information increase. Few providers can yet meet the need for massive investment in information systems, a legacy of the 'good old days' of the NHS where no-one knew what was happening within it.

In London the emphasis has therefore been on annual renewable contracts with little sophistication except, more recently, for 'added value' *i.e.* more work for the same money, or more commonly less money for the same work. This creates a block to any form of strategic planning by hospitals since they cannot plan in the medium term without any idea of their projected income. There has been little attempt yet to enter into a constructive partnership with providers to plan the delivery of services over, say, a three or five year period, thus driving up the quality as promised in the White Paper. Instead annual uncertainty paralyses service development, consultant recruitment and capital investment in equipment and buildings. For example one London purchaser moved their block contract for plastic surgery twice in 1992/3 and again at the start of 1993/4. Another had not allocated its contract for 1994/5 half way through the year!

GPFHs have been shown to have achieved most in improving service provision, perhaps because they understand clinical priorities better or perhaps because they wield greater financial clout. Their relative paucity within London is further to its detriment.

☐ *Allow Greater Choice For GP and Patient*
In the absence of large-scale GP fundholding this objective has clearly failed since the money has not followed the patient, rather the patient has followed a dwindling amount of money held by the DHAs. Patients from less efficient or less wealthy purchasers are beginning to accumulate on waiting lists whilst patients from neighbouring authorities and GPFHs get treated

ahead of them. This is priority by geography rather than clinical need. Whilst it is true that GPs and patients (through the Community Health Councils) have some influence on purchasers' strategies, it is clear nonetheless that most decisions are being driven by fiscal rather than clinical or patient-orientated considerations.

One London DHA chose to place its contract for plastic surgery 30 miles from its population, requiring a frail 87 year old patient to travel to clinics on two buses, a train and a fifteen minute walk when there was a plastic surgery unit just a few minutes away in which he had been treated for many years.

There is no greater evidence for the failure of this objective than the recurring outrage of disenfranchisement of patients on waiting lists at the start of each financial year. Patients already referred to a unit with which there is a contract, by choice and with the recommendation of their GP, seen by the consultant and placed on a waiting list for surgery, suddenly find that this is overridden by the purchaser moving the contract to another provider. The patient is left in limbo on a waiting list from which they cannot be admitted, and faced with having to start all over again somewhere else with the knowledge that the process could be repeated the following April. Some GPs in North London have resorted to referring their patients to three different plastic surgery units from the outset to ensure that when their time comes there will be a contract for treatment.

A recent letter from a GP tells of a young girl with a disfiguring haemangioma referred for plastic surgery to the nearest unit but refused an ECR for outpatients and therefore re-referred by the GP to another hospital. An outpatient appointment date was given there but the contract was withdrawn before she could be seen and the appointment was cancelled. She was seen at a specialist skin hospital fifteen months later who put her on their waiting list for treatment. Since April this would also be an ECR and the purchaser has directed the GP to re-refer her to the original unit with whom (at the moment) there is now a contract. She has already waited 50 months and has yet to be treated. Is this evidence for greater patient or GP choice?

Indeed it is now a moot point to whom a patient 'belongs'. The GP has to refer patients as directed by the purchaser. The consultant is directed by the provider when to see them in the clinic and by the purchaser via the contracting department when to operate on them, irrespective of clinical need. The consultant may find one day that 50 patients on their waiting list have been taken away and put onto someone else's at another hospital without reference to the patient, the consultant, the provider or the GP. Yet the purchaser will not accept clinical responsibility for the consequences of this, saying that it is the clinician's role. As a consultant ENT surgeon recently told his managers when they expressed concern at the length of his waiting list:

I do not have a waiting list any more. I operate on the number of patients that you ask me to each month, be it two or fifty-two. We are performing exactly to contract. It is not my waiting list any more but yours. If you let me decide upon whom and when to operate then it can be mine again.

The very act of getting a patient onto a waiting list and then admitted has become a bureaucratic obstacle course for clinicians. The patient's postcode must be matched to their DHA. The GP must be identified in case they are fundholding. The procedure must be checked to see if it is chargeable to the GP or the DHA. The contract must be scrutinised to ensure that it covers the proposed operation. Sending for the patient for admission requires many more hurdles to clear. An audit of one unit's admission process found 24 different steps were now required before the patient could be sent for. It is difficult to reconcile this with the White Paper's assertion that 'the reforms will make it easier for consultants and their colleagues to get on with the job of treating patients'.[6]

□ *To Encourage Providers to Provide a Better Service to Patients*

There is no doubt that some of the reforms and consequent changes have benefited patients by providing a more responsive service. It was clearly wrong to structure out patients' clinics so that they always ran two hours late and the Patients' Charter has brought pressure to bear over this. Patients being seen for the first time should have the benefit of a consultant opinion, not that of a trainee: this also should help to reduce the number of patients inappropriately on waiting lists and ensure that patients are adequately counselled before engaging in surgery.

Ideally the trainee would be sitting in the clinic learning from the consultant, not in the room across the hall.

GPs (and especially GPFHs) have found, often for the first time, that their views are being sought about the service offered by providers and that their complaints and frustrations are being addressed. 'First impression' teams in hospitals try to see things from a new patient perspective leading to better access and signposting in most hospitals. Rack upon rack of patient information leaflets are *de rigueur* for any provider. The consultant is chastised by outpatient managers for arriving late or running behind and the friends' coffee lounge has been refurbished.

It is clearly better for patients with a condition requiring multi-disciplinary care, such as those with cleft palate or spina bifida, to be seen in a specialised clinic where experts from all disciplines can be seen at the same time, rather than in four or five different clinics. Although the emphasis on service provision has encouraged such initiatives, the purchaser does not always seem to agree. Recently a DHA has tried to direct that a child with a cleft palate have its plastic surgery in the regional unit but post-operative orthodontics in another hospital, preventing joint care by the cleft lip and palate team. A paediatric surgeon caring for a child with spina bifida wanted to refer her to a London teaching hospital with a combined clinic of neurosurgeons, urologists and paediatricians. The purchaser suggested that the child be seen at three different providers, seeing one specialist team in each.

The many requirements and targets that now exist can result in considerable conflict. In plastic surgery there are many patients who would not consider it unreasonable to wait over eight weeks to be seen for their first consultation provided that when the time comes they are seen on time and given an adequate consultation. The charter standard has meant that in order to reduce the routine outpatient appointment delay to less than eight weeks many more patients must be squeezed into each clinic and not all can be seen by a consultant. The clinics become over-full and run late. Creating additional clinics means less time for operating, audit and teaching and more patients to be added to the waiting list each week.

One solution is to refuse some referrals and it is easy to suspect that this may be the intention, thus rationing demand

and reducing expenditure. If in reality the money was following the patient, demand-led providers could afford to expand a unit in response to these pressures. Purchasers, however, set their own agenda and penalise specialties for whom demand exceeds supply.

Many patient initiatives are detrimental to the training of junior doctors. Establishing elective operating lists in the evenings and weekends may suit working patients and optimise theatre usage but unless matched by additional junior staff is a further service burden upon trainees and in conflict with moves to reduce their hours of work. Consultant outreach clinics give GPFH's patients easy access to the specialist but the trainees are usually left behind at the hospital. Expanding peripheral consultant-led operating lists too often mean an unsupervised registrar back in the main unit. Reduced workload in some surgical specialties has reduced the training benefit of many hospital posts at a time when the length of training is proposed to shorten. Greater day-case surgery is attractive but most guidelines require the surgeon and anaesthetist to be a senior registrar or consultant, thus further reducing junior trainees' clinical experience.

Conclusions

The changes in the NHS since 1991 are indeed proving to be 'the most far reaching reform'[7] that the Government predicted. In some aspects of care the NHS is indeed better run, wastage is less and patients and GPs are getting a better deal from the hospital service. The contracting process does not, however, always ensure that 'the patient's needs ... remain paramount'.[8] The abolition of central planning in favour of response to local need places considerable responsibility on purchasers which some are failing to meet. The financial constraints that they are under have led to poorly considered and implemented strategies from which patient care suffers.

The ideology of the purchaser/provider split has often acted as a barrier to purchasers developing services in partnership with hospitals and inter-hospital competition has not always been beneficial to patient or clinician. The ECR system has led to both inequality and iniquity for patients with DHAs putting too little aside for their funding. Last year one DHA had allowed only £15,000 per week for ECRs for all its population: a patient with major burns and another requiring complex surgery would use up several weeks worth of ECR funding. One Sussex DHA had to borrow so much to cover 'unexpected' ECRs in 1993/4 that, after paying back the loan, they had used up their entire budget for 1994/5 by June. This degree of under-funding restricts choice for both patients and doctors and may lead to sub-optimal treatment.

Despite a commitment to medical education in the White Paper, the drive for a more efficient and cost-effective service makes little allowance for training consultants of the future. The true cost of teaching remains unquantified and, whilst hospitals may attract additional money for training medical students, no allowance is made for a consultant getting through less operations in a day when supervising a trainee surgeon.

The reforms have created a public awareness of priorities in health care and how demand may be rationed equitably which is a positive step after decades of covert rationing in the surgery or clinic. It is essential that providers should be involved in the debate and that current *ad hoc* policies developed out of financial desperation in purchasers' offices be subject to scrutiny.

Now the swollen ranks of hospital managers that followed the reforms are being reduced again as budgets becomes ever tighter, despite greater clinical efficiency and hospital closures. What greater evidence could there be for insufficient funding within the reformed NHS?

Notes

1 *Working for Patients*, London: HMSO, January 1989, Para. 1.9, p. 4.

2 *Ibid*, Para. 1.9, pp. 4-5.

3 *Ibid*, Foreword by the Prime Minister.

4 Gudex, C. and Kind, P., *The QUALY Toolkit*, Discussion paper 38, Centre for Health Economics, University of York, 1988.

5 Cole, R.P., Shakespeare, V., Shakespeare, P. and Hobby, J.E.A., 'Measuring Outcome in Low-Priority Plastic Surgery Patients using Quality of Life Indices', *British Journal of Plastic Surgery*, 1994, vol. 47, pp. 117-21.

6 *Working for Patients*, Para. 5.1, p. 39.

7 *Ibid*, Foreword by the Prime Minister.

8 *Ibid,* Foreword by the Prime Minister.

The Effects of the Purchaser/Provider Split on Patient Care

Robert Kennedy and John C. Nicholls

Introduction

In 1986 Professor Alan Maynard proposed that general practitioners might be given the powers to purchase services from hospitals on behalf of their patients.[1] This proposal was taken up and used in the Government's White Paper *Working for Patients* which appeared in 1989.[2] On the inception of the Heath Service in 1948 the basis of funding had been to give resources to hospitals and community services. It was not until the early 1980s that any form of external accountability was deemed necessary. It seemed to the general practitioner that from then on the need for accountability steadily increased until the purchaser/provider split was first introduced, ensuring that all parties worked within a set and fixed budget. The idea that the general practitioner should act as purchaser, advocate and adviser for his patients was for many practices an attractive one, but many others were daunted by the necessarily increased workload of preparation and by the idea of the financial accountability.

To explore the effect of this we have attempted to answer ten questions from the point of view of a purchaser (a first wave GP fundholder) and of a provider (the Medical Director of a fourth wave trust hospital), from the same area and serving the same population. The questions we posed ourselves, in an attempt to analyse the current problems relating to the introduction of the provider/purchaser split, were:

1   Is it an answer to limited resources?

2   Does it place the money in the correct hands?

3   Has it increased bureaucracy at the expense of spending on direct patient care?

4   Has the loss of a monopolistic purchaser led to tiers of services with differing priorities?

5   Is it beneficial to: a)   the patient?
                             b)   the purchaser?
                             c)   the provider?
                             d)   the Government?

6   Does it affect the interrelationships between all parties?

7   Has it clarified who is in charge of the patient's welfare or has it interfered with the doctor/patient relationship?

8   Has it affected clinical practice?

9   Will it benefit strategic planning?

10   Will it survive?

1. Is It the Answer To Limited Resources?

Any country, however wealthy, will find it difficult to meet the health needs of its population. The complexity and therefore the cost of medical care is increasing steadily. There is an unlimited demand which must be met with limited resources. In the United Kingdom there is an almost unique system of primary care. The general practitioner is trusted by patients and is able to advise them on the appropriateness of treatment. In the words of Professor Maynard: 'the family doctor was, in the British system, a patient adviser and guide, through the whole complex system of health care and why not give him or her the financial power to act on behalf of the patient'.[3] The Government had long seen general practitioners as the gatekeepers of health care and this gatekeeping had previously been carried out on the basis of clinical need. Now that money is part of the equation the general practitioners' decision-making process needs to be further refined, as the balance sheet now starkly identifies where the money is being spent. In practice this has not been a serious difficulty as yet. Patients have continued to enjoy the choice between hospitals and/or consultants as before the reforms and there has not been a need to withhold treatment where it is genuinely appropriate.

From the general practitioner's perspective therefore it may be seen to be a reasonable way to share out fairly the limited resources, and to the provider the purchaser/provider split concept does provide an uncomfortable answer. However, it raises a number of ethical dilemmas. The provider can set an agenda of what can be provided within the resource package, but in

practice the provider needs to take on board the purchasers'
wishes and may not be able to control demand (e.g. the emergency workload is unpredictable). 'Non-income' generating health
problems may not form part of the provider package so who then
treats these patients?

It allows the purchaser to set priorities but the provider may
not be able to match these in terms of the facilities available.
There will often be a time lag if the provider needs additional
facilities to meet the demands. By developing a sound business
case, however, there is a sharpening up of future resource
commitment. Additional requirements for training/research/audit
etc. can be built into the contract price, but this can mean that
the cost becomes uncompetitive and thus there is an element of
risk in any development proposal.

The provider will not be the determiner of the range of
services and may be faced with being required to provide
services which are uneconomic in order to ensure the viability of
the unit. The interdependence of the various specialities will
cause the provider to make such provision even if it is not fully
funded.

Despite these problems we are probably beginning to provide
a service which is more sensitive to our purchasers' (GP and
District Health Authority) requirements. This is happening
despite the serious misgivings in terms of a two-tier service (see
below).

2. Does it Put the Money in the Right Hands?

General practices are small businesses within which the partners
have been accountable and responsible to each other. They have
in many instances funded and developed their own premises.
Health care in the United Kingdom consumes a smaller fraction
of the gross national product than almost any other developed
country and the general practitioner system has contributed a
great deal to this state of affairs. The drug expenditure per
capita is low and the effective use of secondary and tertiary care
is high. Further examples of this are the conservative use of
elective surgery, the rational use of investigations and the
continuous assessment of outcomes so that expensive treatment
is not continued to the detriment of the patients. It would
therefore seem reasonable to place resources in the hands of the

GP fundholders. Thus for them the answer is probably yes; but as yet the purchasing consortia (mainly health agencies) are in some difficulty for they are often perceived as being visionary, politically directed, self interested, and poorly informed. For these reasons the provider looks with great suspicion upon the way in which these purchasing consortia are apportioning the money.

The provider does not have any money as of right: it has to be earned. This fits well with the concept of the money following patients, which providers supported, but that is not yet happening. The reasons for this appear to be threefold. There is a restricted list of funded procedures and thus extra activity may not be rewarded: this applies mostly to GP fundholder (GPFH) activity. There is no direct relation of income to the volume of emergency work. Lastly, the provider may not be able to choose which services it wishes to provide, and may be forced (by financial pressures) into what appears to be spending money unwisely.

A further problem is that planning becomes uncertain for there is no guarantee of income. This has been aggravated by the cynicism created in the distribution of money to the GPFHs which previously had been apportioned to the provider (i.e. it is seen as 'our' money). Considerable suspicion has been aroused as to how the size of these budgets was determined.

It is widely believed that GPFHs, and indeed Health Authorities, hold back something like 20 per cent of their allocation for contingencies whilst expecting the provider to increase activity levels. Similarly 'efficiency' savings cut across the concept of earning money by activity, especially when these are demanded in the middle of the financial year (e.g. nationally agreed pay rises/Government-imposed cost improvement programmes etc).

One positive development that has occurred as a result of the balance sheet mentality has been that providers have looked to widen the area from which to draw their patient flows, even though this can lead to an unhealthy rivalry between providers. The patient can benefit from this.

3. Has it Increased Bureaucracy with a Resulting Increase in the Non-Direct Patient Care Costs?

Practices which embraced fundholding were provided with a start-up grant and then a management allowance which was initially £30,000 per year and has been indexed to inflation. This is a strictly limited budget for management and it can therefore be seen that any increase in bureaucracy is minimal. (A management fee of £30,000 on a budget of between £1-2 million must be minimalist in cost but it does work.) There are, of course, other management fees incurred at the FHSA and the Region but these are more difficult to evaluate. Full computer-isation has been of great benefit, reducing bureaucracy at the general practice level.

From the provider's viewpoint there appears to have been an enormous increase in the bureaucratic processes necessary to initiate, run and monitor the management aspects of the split. Provider units have had to establish whole departments mainly to undertake contract negotiations and monitoring which are entirely new. The business planning process is not strictly innovative but has been sharpened up at the cost of creation of a cadre of business managers which are also new. A medical management hierarchy has been established which, unlike previously, has managerial accountability. To meet these demands clinical sessions have been relinquished, taking those clinicians away from direct patient care.

Additionally, and sadly, there has been no perceptible lessening of outside pressures and accountability to 'higher' agencies e.g. NHS Management Executive/Regions/Outposts/Post-graduate educational bodies etc., all of which need to be serviced.

The extra contractual referral (ECR) system is seen as a valuable source of income, but the bureaucracy involved has on several occasions been seen to interfere with clinical care.

The expansion of health services managers together with the proliferation of paper or computer generated transactions are seen by many providers as the worst effect of the purchaser/provider split, and are constantly cited as a reason why direct patient care has been compromised.

4. Has the Change from Monolithic Purchaser Led to Several Tiers of Service with Differing Priorities?

The main political criticism of the fundholding principle has been that it establishes two tiers of service. The GP author would contend that there have always been many tiers of service and that if fundholding was to prove anything it had to allow certain essential freedoms to the fundholding practice. During the first year there were strong pressures to maintain 'steady state'. After the first year there was considerable encouragement to be innovative and flexible. The freedom to refer where and when it was in the patient's best interests and the flexibility to transfer some secondary care back into the primary care setting were felt equally necessary. With these two advantages, freedom and flexibility, the fundholding practice was able to deal with its long waiters for secondary care and to improve its own in-house services. In this respect the smaller unit of a practice or group of practices has a great advantage over the large District Health Authority. The reduction in waiting lists was largely achieved by using providers who had marginal over-capacity rather than establishing a two tier system with their immediate local providers. My partners have not sought priority as fundholders rather than on clinical considerations. They regret that uncomfortable pressures have been placed on some hospital clinicians to favour fundholders. On several occasions they have co-funded local waiting list initiatives with the District Health Authority. For the provider the range of purchasers has clearly led to conflicts of interest. The major conflict is between clinical and financial priority, with the former still (fortunately) being dominant. However, where an equivalent clinical problem is presented, there is a clear two-tier level of care whereby the directly financed patient receives priority. In a broader context there may be conflict between contracts if special deals have been made with different purchasers. This is particularly difficult if private sector facilities are purchased and a consultant within the provider unit is asked to take on the treatment. A conflict of loyalties clearly arises.

It has been suggested that when all GPs have fundholding status this conflict will be eliminated, but this will only occur if the resources are adequate, and all procedures/treatments are funded. At present, with approximately 70 per cent of our GP referrals coming from fundholding practices, the dilemmas are lessened, but we are already struggling with the problem of which services are properly and adequately funded.

With the anxiety to achieve financial stability there has been a tendency to separate waiting lists by financial criteria, sometimes without clinical input, leading to obvious suspicion. The clinicians obviously need to be very closely involved with the drawing up of contracts and the determination of priorities for treatment, but as yet the systems devised have not fully allowed this to happen.

5. Has it Proved Beneficial to The Patient, The Purchasers, The Providers, The Government?

There is absolutely no doubt that in the GP author's practice the patients have benefited greatly. Long waiters have been dealt with and in-house services have been greatly improved and extended.

The provider, however, has needed to ensure income by selecting directly funded patients for treatment at the expense of others. To offset this, the limits to which the provider has been subjected may have restricted overall choice for the patient. By classifying patients into managed units of work the individual care for each patient can be affected. There may be earlier or even inappropriate discharge to secure the expected activity levels, and tertiary referrals may have been limited by financial considerations.

Overall the provider has become cost conscious and, in order to meet the global targets, the patient may be compromised. There could be a tendency for inappropriate care, or even unnecessary operations. At present these pessimistic scenarios do not seem to have taken place but even the monitoring by purchasers has not indicated any tangible benefits experienced by patients receiving secondary care.

Provider status has led to a sharpening up of medical audit, and the introduction of patient satisfaction surveys, which may be beneficial to the patient.

The purchasers have learnt a great deal by the experience and improved their skills, particularly with contracting and forward planning. They have relished the freedom and flexibility that has been granted to them. In a health service which has been seen to be under continual political criticism, the fund-holder has been able to work with enthusiasm delivering health care with choice. The providers will answer this question with more poignancy but the fundholders would suggest that they have benefited in several ways. Where there was over-capacity this has been used, and they have been able to run more efficiently. Specific services have been set up to help the patient and closer co-operation between purchaser and provider and analysis of outcome has enabled priorities to be established.

The providers see obvious benefits for the purchaser, but there appear to be perceptible benefits to the provider as well.

Management roles are now more clearly defined, with accountability and responsibility more overt. Processes of outcome measurements are moving forward; and a competitive element amongst neighbouring providers has emerged (not always a benefit). These have been achieved however with much effort put into review and revision of services leading to a significant reorganisation (which at present is at an undetermined cost to the taxpayer).

The Government has benefited in that fundholding has been shown to work. General practitioner fundholders have been shown to be responsible and efficient, in short good housekeepers and good gatekeepers. But there is a hidden agenda in that the Government has managed to devolve responsibility down to the purchasers and providers. This particularly applies to the difficult decisions in relation to limited resources.

The establishment of trusts has enabled political input nearer the grassroots by selection of trust board members. Providers expect that once accurate figures are obtained the suggested inefficiencies and waste in the NHS may not be quite so widespread and large as the Government had predicted.

6. Does it Improve or Worsen Inter-Relationships Between All Parties Concerned Including the Patient?

Undoubtedly there have been some disadvantages to fundholding. It has been seen as élitist, divisive within the profession, and patients have seen it as a threat to themselves should they require expensive and complex medical care. There is an implied threat to the good relationships between GPs and hospital consultants. In practice it has certainly not been possible to resolve all these factors. However, the practice concerned feels it has brought closer liaison with the secondary care providers. Regular meetings with key clinicians, hospital managers and the community care team leaders, have improved the understanding between the various parties. Further expansion of fundholding to include other and smaller practices as a consortium have ironed out some of the difficulties.

Inevitably misunderstandings have arisen because of the reforms, but there has been a considerable degree of team building. Trust (in both senses) creation has yet to be proven to be working.

Within the provider unit there can be unhealthy competition with conflicts arising, often around the two-tier issues.

Further difficulties have arisen by the stark separation into purchaser or provider of former colleagues who worked within a single health authority.

7. Has it Affected the Doctor/Patient Relationship?

The doctor/patient relationship is a delicate one. In the UK it has particular advantages. If the patient's expectations remain reasonable, then the responsible doctor is able to meet them. There are some grey areas: cosmetic surgery, sports injuries and psychotherapy are good examples. While budgets remain adequate and expectations remain reasonable the system will work. Great emphasis has been placed on the gatekeeping role but, on reflection, perhaps it is the conservative attitude of the population which has enabled the system to work. There is not a rush to try the untested, to be a guinea pig or to radically change lifestyle. While the doctor must remain in charge, as he has the responsibility, the patients have also accepted responsibility themselves. The doctor/patient relationship remains good.

With the provider doctor there is a degree of confusion amongst patients as to their status due to lack of understanding of the reforms, and this can add a new dimension to some consultations. The impact of both politically-led (e.g. Patients' Charter) and media-led campaigns can cause face-to-face conflict between doctor and patient in trying to explain the changes which the split has brought about.

The 'price-on-the-head' syndrome may be felt by both parties and, although this is not yet interfering with clinical decisions, it may do so as it becomes more overt. This will be particularly liable to happen towards the end of the contract period.

The increased expectation of the patient, and the often severe constraints felt by the provider, have clearly affected this delicate relationship. If clinical decisions are thought to be increasingly affected by overriding managerial considerations then this will have a further detrimental effect.

8. Has it Affected Clinical Practice?

It is tempting to say No, but the honest answer is in all probability a qualified Yes. Once the cost of secondary care procedures is known to the advising general practitioner it must influence his clinical management in the same way that, once the awareness of the cost of certain drugs is known, the way in which they are prescribed is modified. This is an area in which many non-fundholding practices made their stand. They felt the Government should take the responsibility of funding or not funding treatment, and that their practices should not be confined by a set budget. This view was totally understandable but unrealistic. In the GP author's practice clinical management has, in fact, improved over the course of three years of fund-holding, in particular with more rapid access to secondary care.

It is also worth emphasising the fact that clinical practice is constantly changing and will always be constantly changing. New practices evolve and old practices are discarded. Endoscopic surgery is steadily gaining acceptance and is actually cheaper; mentally ill patients are less likely to be incarcerated for life in expensive institutions. The whole picture is constantly changing and is a stimulating one.

Provider practices in general have not at present been greatly affected. As previously mentioned, the medical audit process has been sharpened; but still the audit cycle is not necessarily being completed. The lowering of length of stay of patients and the extension of day surgery facilities was already occurring through changing clinical practice, and has not been greatly influenced by the split.

There has been an element of cross speciality suspicion, with the more accurate monitoring of performance which has become necessary as part of the contract process. Perhaps as a result of this, clinical teams are concentrating on drawing up guidelines and protocols which may gradually have a more distinct impact on clinical practice.

9. Does Strategic Planning Benefit or Suffer?

It is accepted that there is a very different planning agenda for the provider compared with the purchaser. As already stated, in the first year of fundholding most practices felt confined to a steady state and felt that if they weren't they would cause chaos to their local providers. For example, if they took large areas of their activity away from local provision, e.g. pathology, orthopaedic surgery or ophthalmic surgery, the local services would be in danger of collapse. So long as close liaison is maintained with local providers, service can only improve. Regular meetings, appropriate contracts, planning, and co-purchasing with the district are essential. Nevertheless, the poor provider will eventually suffer loss of contracts and this will always remain a contentious and uncomfortable area for the purchaser who may feel responsible for the failure of a provider unit.

The provider, however, has benefited by being able to define the resources available more accurately, and evaluating future services linked to adequate income. Demand still exceeds available resources, and will always do so, but once money truly follows the patient a more realistic planning process may be facilitated.

By drawing the clinical teams together through the business planning process overall strategic planning has probably become easier (as has operational planning). Trusts are probably now better informed than were previous health provider units, which should improve the planning process.

10. Will It/Should It Continue?

Fundholding work with small accountable units would seem to deliver good health care. They are flexible, they can be innovative and they can improve the general standards for all. It may be disruptive to local strategic planning but it should not be. It has been extended to cover community services, may soon cover obstetric services, and in the future would hopefully cover acute services. To date there have been safety nets, for example with the expensive patient, and provided these are maintained to cover that type of patient, then all services could become fundholding. There has been a steady increase in the number of fundholding practices and, provided commitment remains voluntary, it is hoped that this will continue.

As a final plea, the GP author expresses his concern that if fundholders are persuaded to form large groups they will lack individuality and flexibility. Small accountable units have been seen to work and there are direct parallels with this in industry. The fundholding concept was untried and untested but in practice it has delivered medical care and choice while remaining financially accountable.

The providers see its continuation as inevitable—almost by default. There are the beginnings of an acceptance of the fundamental changes that have been introduced. This has probably been assisted by the realisation that clinical practice has not been adversely affected. The providers always supported the concept of money following work and outcomes (not just activity) and in some acute specialities this does appear to be happening.

Concentration on the provision of specific services, rather than the broader concept of total care which was previously expected, has helped providers. As the purchaser's role becomes clearer this will continue to improve.

Notes

1   Maynard, A., 'Performance Incentives', in Teeling Smith, G., (ed.), *Health Education and General Practice*, London: Office of Health Economics, 1986, pp. 44-46.

2   *Working for Patients*, White Paper presented to Parliament by the Secretaries of State for Health, Wales, Northern Ireland and Scotland, London: HMSO, January 1989.

3   Maynard, A., *op. cit.*

Further Reading

The Department of Health, *Funding General Practice: the Programme for the Introduction of GP Budgets*, London: HMSO, 1989.

Glennerster, H., *A Foothold for Fundholding: A Preliminary Report on the Introduction of GP Fundholding*, King's Fund Institute, 1992.

To Budget or Not To Budget?
The Experience of a Non-Budgeting General Practice

Gillian and Ben FitzGerald

This Hertfordshire non-budgeting practice operates from main premises in Radlett with outlying surgeries at Park Street and Shenley. Six general practitioners serve 14,000 patients with an auxiliary staff of one practice manager, 2 full-time (ft) nurses, 1 part-time (pt), 2 secretaries (1 ft, 1 pt) and 14 receptionist clerks (1 ft and 10 pt at main surgery; 3 pt at Park Street surgery and none at Shenley).

The main surgery, a two storey house at the centre of Radlett, was recently substantially upgraded. There is a large waiting room alongside the reception and records area, with adjacent toilets. Four consulting rooms are situated on the ground floor with two treatment rooms for the practice nurses and there are two further consulting rooms on the first floor with two offices for the practice manager and book-keeper/secretary.

The purchasing authority is the Hertfordshire Health Agency in Welwyn Garden City. There have been meetings with the Agency Purchasing Adviser since the NHS reforms but the practice has minimal influence on purchasing decisions.

Prior to the start of the new system our patients could be referred to virtually any district general hospital, and to any of the London undergraduate or specialist hospitals; also, if and when specially desired, to any other accessible provincial hospital.

But now the majority of our district hospital referrals for consultation, or for emergency and elective treatment, are to

---

This paper was prepared and agreed following a discussion amongst the six practice partners, Dr C.M. Maxwell, Dr S.B. FitzGerald, Dr G.M. FitzGerald, Dr I.G. Gold, Dr M.J. Ingram and Dr P.K. Sweeney, and the practice manager Mrs Barbara Hilton.

Watford General Hospital, with smaller numbers going to St Albans, Barnet and Edgware.

In regard to the London undergraduate hospitals we can now only refer our patients to St Mary's and the Royal Free (generally, although not invariably, for more specialised care), and we are no longer able to use the Middlesex Hospital, Barts and St Thomas'. Of the London postgraduate and specialist hospitals we can refer patients to St Mark's, Moorfields, Hammersmith, and the National Hospitals for Nervous Diseases. Some idea of the wide range of contracting by the Hertfordshire Health Agency can be gauged from a chart which it publishes giving details of 28 specialties at some 37 different hospitals serving patients of non-fundholding general practitioners in the county.

The cancellation of contracts with the Royal National Orthopaedic at Stanmore, the Middlesex, St Thomas' and Barts during 1994 is a matter of concern for all of us and has upset many of our patients.

Referrals to other specialist hospitals and more specialised departments are more difficult and there are many problems in regard to extra-contractual referrals (ECRs). For example, earlier this year the daughter of a retired doctor was easily referred for a particular endoscopic (non-cosmetic) operation under local anaesthesia by a plastic surgeon at Charing Cross Hospital, but the purchasing authority no longer allows use of this specialist. Therefore, our NHS patients are denied the benefits of such treatment although private patients (as, in our opinion, should be the case for *all* patients) can, of course, go to this same surgeon.

On the more positive side we can report one recently successful ECR to the specialist unit of our choice of a young lady with anorexia nervosa. This entailed a special application to the purchasing authority before approval was given. Of course, had we been a budgeting practice, we ourselves, instead of the Hertfordshire Health Agency, could have made the decision. Nevertheless, in the context of many other similar judgements about a wide variety of ECRs, this patient's condition would still have required careful consideration of competing claims on available resources. Whether or not it would have been any easier to arrange this referral, had we been a budgeting practice, we cannot say. However, in our experience there is often a two-tier health service due to preferential purchasing and, sometimes, to actual queue-jumping for consultations and/or admission, largely dependent upon the availability of funding from different purchasers as well as the pressing financial needs of some providers. This is supported by colleagues in other non-funding practices.

It may be asked, what have been the financial implications for our practice? As individual practitioners our earnings have not been directly affected by the purchaser/provider system. However, the doctors' total practice income has increased substantially because of unrelated changes in remuneration for various items of service such as meeting immunisation and cervical cytology targets which are generally more easily achieved with a better educated clientele such as we serve. The salary of non-medical practice staff has not been affected in this way since their earnings are determined by Whitley scales. Staff reimbursement from governmental funds varies between 50 and 100 per cent of total salary whilst the remainder is paid as a practice expense by deduction from the six partners' gross income.

It is interesting to compare non-medical staff salaries in different types of practice. Currently, salaries of such full-time staff in a non-fundholding practice vary between £15,000 and £19,000, the practice manager generally being the highest paid. However, managers in some fundholding practices are earning up to £29,000 per annum. Were we to be fundholders this practice would need at least two more offices and two to three additional full-time staff. Our own work load has increased exponentially, partly due to the increased collection of data and also due to the preparation of more letters of referral as a result of increased consumer demand.

Without having ourselves experienced the general practice budgeting system we believe that our advantages in a non-fundholding practice are:-

☐ Less bureaucracy
☐ Less stress
☐ Less friction within the partnership.

First, there is less bureaucracy within the practice because, for better or worse, we have to rely on the Hertfordshire Agency for contractual decisions. In the event of any of us wishing to make an extra-contractual referral (ECR), we must first know where we wish to send the patient and then apply to the Hertfordshire Agency. Of course, the Agency may decline to allow the ECR on budgetary or other grounds and then the problem is back in our court. We can either accept the decision or make a further determined appeal to the Agency. Sometimes the patient may decide to break the bureaucratic barrier by opting for private treatment, an option which is clearly not open to everyone even in this relatively well-to-do residential area. With less bureaucracy we have more time for our patients and lower administrative costs as less computer equipment is needed. Moreover, although we are subjected to scrutiny and advice regarding our prescribing costs, there is as yet no actual financial limit applied to us. Our prescribing decisions are still made primarily on perceived clinical need and only secondarily on cost. Referrals are now made to a smaller number of hospitals than in previous years. However, we still feel we have a wide choice of hospitals and with some of these access is now actually easier than hitherto.

Secondly, we believe that there is less stress within the practice because we ourselves are not compelled to make difficult decisions about what could sometimes be irreconcilable clinical priorities. There is certainly less stress between the partners who, whatever they may think of the policies of the Hertfordshire Health Agency, are never involved in intra-practice disputes about contracts and related funding decisions. But, in saying that, we do not imply that we are indifferent to the hard economic facts of life because, like all general practitioners, we have been subject to comparative prescribing costings for many years past. However, we prefer to concentrate primarily on our patients' clinical needs, unfettered by budgetary judgements. This less stressful ambience emphatically suits our partnership's practice ideology.

Thirdly, with less opportunity for friction between the doctors we are more easily able to maintain a happy partnership. Moreover, we believe that this happier doctor/doctor relationship is reflected in a more secure patient/doctor relationship. It is noteworthy that some elderly and other potentially more expensive new patients, on applying to the practice, do sometimes enquire whether we are a budgeting practice. Many of these patients have gained the impression, rightly or wrongly, that they are more likely to be rejected by a fundholding practice.

But certain disadvantages of a non-fundholding practice must also be listed. First, we get no reimbursement for computer systems. Secondly, it has been proven that our patients often get a second-rate service in regard to outpatient appointments and hospital waiting lists: such differential treatment of patients from different practices most certainly did not occur prior to the NHS reforms. Thirdly, we receive less money per patient than do fundholders. Fourthly, there is little help when improving our facilities and services such as, for example, in updating our premises. Lastly we receive no money for in-house ancillary help, e.g. in the provision of physiotherapy or counselling services, which is possible for those fundholders with adequate budgets. Despite these disadvantages we still prefer to remain as a non-fundholding practice, firmly believing that the honeymoon period for the fundholders will almost certainly be followed by ever-tightening financial controls.

Perhaps the most striking difference between the new purchaser/provider system and private specialist referral is that, in the new NHS the patient now follows the money, whereas, in the private sector, the money follows the patient. That being so, when we are asked the $60,000 question—'would you prefer to return to the former conditions of NHS practice?'—we all tend to reply with an emphatic 'yes'.

The Impact of the NHS Reforms on Patient Care
A View from a London Teaching Hospital

Geoffrey Glazer

Introduction

Generalisations about the National Health Service are difficult to make, given its size and diversity, and any comments or criticisms made by those working within the service are usually purely subjective. However, individuals like myself working as a consultant in the acute field of general surgery in a London teaching hospital can hopefully convey an impression of the impact of the NHS reforms within their own sphere.

The purchaser/provider split has induced major changes in the delivery of health care. These changes are continuing at a rapid pace and are occurring simultaneously with other professional developments. There are, for example, changes in the training and service regulations of junior doctors, changes in Continuing Medical Education (CME), more detailed audits and reviews of clinical practice, all set against a backdrop of an increasingly difficult medico-legal situation.

Conventional wisdom about the NHS before the current reforms suggested that it was a giant, lumbering, inefficient organisation, somewhat akin to a nationalised industry in an old communist East European state. There were wide variations of practice within the NHS and a fairly high degree of wastage, both on the purchasing side and on the 'shop floor'. This was said to stem from weak management and a total lack of financial control and appreciation of costs. On the positive side, however, it was a professionally led clinical service with a sense of purpose and dedication. The goodwill that existed amongst the vast majority of staff stemmed from a feeling of 'ownership' which, in the hospital service, permeated down from the senior consultants to all other staff and resulted in a service with an ethos of pride and hard work. This goodwill factor persisted despite repeated rebuffs on annual pay awards which gradually eroded the position of health care workers. Broadly speaking the patients were satisfied (waiting lists excepted) and made few complaints.

The cost of the service has always been low, consuming just 6.6 per cent of GDP, and, apart from Japan, the cheapest in the developed world. Doctors salaries were (and remain) low when compared with other professional groups in the UK or doctors in Europe and the USA. Nurses and others were similarly affected by relatively low pay and, as salaries are a major component of NHS costs, the overall service was kept under some financial control.

Demands for increased funding were, however, made on a regular basis, often accompanied by a certain amount of shroud waving by doctors and others. Politicians faced adverse publicity when refusing to meet this insatiable demand. Events were brought to a climax when the three Presidents of the major Royal Colleges (Surgeons, Physicians and Obstetricians & Gynaecologists) came down from their position on the high moral ground of professionalism to confront the Prime Minister directly over funding. This was the final straw for Margaret Thatcher who then set in motion the process of reforms which were introduced a year or so later.

Transferring the Costs

The basic plan of the reforms was to transfer the ever increasing costs of health care (costs compounded by new technologies, an increasingly aged population and generally greater patient expectations) from the Exchequer and, by some process of reorganisation, to pass them on elsewhere, whilst at the same time sustaining the fundamental tenet of the service as being free at the point of delivery. As an attempt to control expenditure and to improve efficiency the reforms seem so far to have been partly successful, according to the Government. This is difficult to quantify as accurate statistics are hard to obtain and the cost of this 'success' has yet to be assessed in terms of the type and standard of service that will remain. The consequences of the reforms have not been thought through and there is a conflict between the new free market forces and the central control and planning which government still imposes. There is the distinct impression that the service is being flown by the seat of its pants and few at trust level are in a position to either predict or plan with any degree of certainty. A coherent strategy is missing, unless the absence of strategy is in itself the policy, and market forces and creeping privatisation are the way of the future.

As a political diversion the reforms have been very successful and the spotlight has been turned away from the government to the purchasers who, by virtue of the fact that they are under-funded, have turned the heat onto the provider. As a means of neutralising the authority of the hospital consultants and associated professions, the reforms have also been an unqualified success, but the goodwill factor has been dissipated.

Is Patient Care Efficient?

One of the fundamental questions arising from the purchaser/ provider split is whether it has resulted in any improvements in patient care. It is easy to lose sight of this issue, which is after all the *raison d'etre* of the Health Service. Patient care is a nebulous concept, but may be considered in terms of clinical outcomes and the promptness and sensitivity of the service being offered. The constant organisational changes and the state of uncertainty which these engender, the stream of management directives which emanate at all levels in the Health Service, and the government's preoccupation with its rather simplistic Patients' Charter, do little to address the basic issues of patient care. All this may be seen as a smoke screen which obscures the underlying fact that the Health Service is not receiving adequate funding from the government. Rather, it is being squeezed at all levels to become more cost-effective and efficient, an ideal that can hardly be challenged, but one which, if driven too far, may have adverse clinical effects and be detrimental to good and safe practice.

How can efficiency impinge on patient care? A major manage-rial efficiency drive is devoted to 'skill-mix' analysis, which inevitably means replacing higher paid and more highly trained staff by cheaper and less skilled workers, or not replacing them at all. The main thrust at the moment is in nursing and other ancillary areas, and this makes sound commercial sense for managers desperate to save money. Sometimes it may be justified if, for example, it releases trained nursing staff from non-nursing clerical duties on the wards. In other areas the result is not always so acceptable in that some professional work such as nursing in outpatients does require a level of expertise that is not apparent to non-clinical managers. The experienced nurse who knew the patients, their clinical and other problems and who was trained and prepared to deal with their wound dressings, injections, intimate examinations and so forth is being supplanted by a transient, untrained individual with no experience. The counselling and support offered by the old fashioned nurse to a patient in distress is not something easily measured and certainly not available from their untrained successors. Cheaper yes, but one doubts that it is better. Elsewhere, when nurses have stood out for clinical standards they have been removed. In other ancillary fields such as physiotherapy and social work the impact has been to reduce staffing levels.

The final group designated for skill-mix review is the medical profession. This is a harder nut to crack than others but one which some managers are prepared to tackle with relish. There is a carrot and stick approach; in some cases senior consultants have been tempted by increased benefits to take early retirement, whilst in others there have been enforced redundancies. Early retirement certainly lowers costs and also allows the possibility of a cheaper replacement to be appointed, usually with a new style of contract which may be more restrictive and may state, for example, that any private practice of the appointee must be carried out within the facilities of the hospital (if they exist), thus increasing the trust's income. The extent of this loss of consultant expertise is difficult to measure and it may be argued that younger consultants will bring a modern approach to their practice. However, there are instances where a senior consultant has been forced to retire only to find himself reappointed on a part time basis because there was no one with his specialist skills to carry on his work.

The quality of the service on offer will be one of the predominant issues of the future, and there are conflicting pressures on managers. On the one hand the financial pressure could lead to more sub-consultant posts or even non-medical personnel taking over certain clinical roles, whereas on the other there is the demand of purchasers for a consultant based service. The Royal Colleges, in their role as guardians of clinical standards, are determined to maintain the consultant's position as the team leader. Unfortunately the number of consultants is insufficient to adequately cover all the exigencies demanded by the service. Thus, if the purchaser wishes to have consultants to do all the operating in the Day Care Unit, this can only be done by reducing their workload elsewhere or by employing more consultants.

A cheap alternative for managers is to appoint doctors of sub-consultant grade to posts with either a limited tenure or with a limited clinical remit. This temptation is encouraged by the tendency to fragment clinical practice into a disease or symptom 'clinic' and by the availability of willing and otherwise unemployed medical personnel. Staffing hospitals with such doctors is, on the surface, cost effective and giving them a restricted role within, for example, a hernia clinic, a varicose vein clinic or some other 'one-stop' clinic is a trend that is developing. Whether sub-consultant doctors can perform as well as consultants in the out-patient or operating theatre has yet to be determined. It may be that within a restricted field of hernia repair or varicose vein surgery they could do better than the transient junior doctor who now commonly performs these sorts of clinical tasks. However, there have been reports of doctors of doubtful ability being employed for short term waiting list initiatives on patients with hernias, which resulted in very poor outcomes and a large medico-legal bill for the trust involved.

The Royal Colleges and the regional postgraduate deans are responsible for the supervision of junior doctor training and thus exert another pressure on managers. The training and service aspects of medicine were always incompatible in the sense that the bulk of routine clinical tasks, with low training value, were carried out by junior doctors. This will cease to a large extent in the future as the hours of duty are reduced and the training becomes more strictly controlled. Already, even at the most junior house-officer level, there are many prohibited tasks such as the routine clerking in of patients for certain operations or the routine taking of blood samples. The trust managers are thus forced to adopt alternative measures to cover these circumstances. If these regulations become too onerous, managers could withdraw from the system entirely and employ doctors from abroad. This was considered by one trust chief executive who, after having an adverse report on his house-officer posts, threatened to fly in a group of German doctors to fill their place.

The Threat to Training

The fact that the postgraduate deans currently have control over 50 per cent of junior doctors' salaries is seen as a means by which training can be safeguarded: withdrawal of funding from an errant trust is a powerful weapon. This may add to the desire of managers to employ doctors who are out of the training system on strict and cheap terms, even if they lose some of this central funding. This managerial move is already being challenged by the BMA and other medical organisations, whose added fear is that if the new Calman system of medical training becomes operational (a residency style of shortened training leading to a specialty qualification) then a further group of doctors unable to find consultant posts will be released into this market. In some specialties (like surgery) the level of knowledge and experience of these doctors will be below that now expected of a newly appointed consultant and the temptation will be to appoint into a sub-consultant grade.

The new training system will also see the reduction in the number of British graduate trainees and their place will have to be filled by staff grade doctors whose standards will be variable. The exact number of reductions to be made to the current levels of registrars and senior registrars has not been announced and estimates vary from 30 per cent to 50 per cent. Some specialties will be able to cope with this but the acute clinical specialties will face enormous difficulties in dealing with the workload.

The situation is aggravated by new regulations governing the hours of work of junior doctors. These new rules, whilst being sensible and humane, do have knock-on cost implications for managers and for clinical standards. Cover can only be maintained by cross specialty arrangements which do not allow continuity of care. The concept of shift work for junior doctors may work well in some service departments like radiology or pathology but does not work well in clinical specialties. The long held principle that a doctor is responsible for his patient is destroyed and the standard of care is reduced. These changes are happening now and it is common practice to find wards covered at weekends by young doctors who do not know the full details of the complex patients under their care.

It is not possible to predict from this scenario what the final effect of the new training system will be on the standard of patient care but the change will be dramatic. The question is confused by the idea that matters will improve as there will be more consultant involvement; that is, a change from a consultant-led to a consultant-based service. However, this cannot occur without more consultants and no such expansion has been agreed by the Government. The annual expansion of the consultant numbers is no more than 2 per cent, but consultant numbers need to increase by 10 per cent per annum for several years to cover the cuts in junior staff envisaged by the Calman system of training (even though the precise numbers are unclear).

Consultants in Chambers?

There are other increasing demands being placed on consultants, with more administration and dedicated time for audit, teaching and CME. This pressure has led to the suggestion that consultants should opt out of the system completely and form chambers, like barristers, in order to sell their services to trusts. This is now being debated seriously, particularly amongst specialties with high earning capabilities. The true worth of the consultant would then be open to market forces. Some have argued that this would be far higher than managers anticipate[1] and certainly higher than current salaries. The need for properly trained and experienced consultants will be further enhanced by the developing medico-legal situation and the propensity for patients to sue. This problem is the hidden time-bomb facing providers (and the Government), with a ten-fold increase in litigation over the last 10 years and an exponential explosion in claims in the last three years.

There are many tensions between managers and consultants, one of which is that managers have little control over the way doctors spend money on individual patients. Judged by commercial standards this is unusual, but in fact there are increasing controls on doctors stemming from the gatekeeper role of management, which sets the contracts and the provision of facilities such as beds or operating time. In terms of clinical practice, consultants are being moulded by managers who would like to see standardised (cheap?) protocols of management introduced. It is possible to lay down anticipated recovery pathways (ARPs) for some basic conditions, usually surgical rather than medical, and such information can be used not only for costing but for managerial audit of clinical practice.

Consultants are often under attack by very outspoken critics like Professor Maynard of the Health Economics Unit of York

University. He sees the main problem in the NHS as the dominance of the clinician and the solution as the transfer of clinical control to health managers and economists. His regard for the intellectual capacity and skills of clinicians is low and his view was shared by at least one chairman of a large trust who spoke publicly in derisive terms about his own consultants, an action which resulted in a unanimous vote of no confidence by his medical staff, followed by his resignation.

Naturally most doctors would reject Maynard's view but they must recognise that the medical profession has to convey, via its audit procedures, a clearer message about its clinical policies and outcomes. There is a common ground here with politicians and managers who are looking for effective treatments. The difficulty lies in the definition of effectiveness and in the methods of testing this in a rigorous and scientific way, whether this applies to a clearcut disease process like a heart attack,[2] or the more nebulous subject of palliative care services.[3] There are also great difficulties in the production of clinical guidelines.[4] Taken to their extreme, these protocols could stifle clinical initiatives, increase non-professional interference, encourage an ever-expanding bureaucracy and lead to legal repercussions.

Too Expensive to Treat

There is a further unresolved ethical issue which lies behind the clinical/cost-effective guidelines that are being set. As more sophisticated pricing develops these guidelines could become a rationing system, and patients could be denied treatment because of the cost. Some would argue that, as no alternative rationing system has been developed, this would be a reasonable path to follow. Rationing has always occurred, but usually the decision was based on clinical rather than economic considerations and many doctors would have grave misgivings about such a step. So would the public, as was evident from the outcry when a London intensive care consultant tentatively suggested that predictive scores of the severity of illness might be used to withhold treatment from those unlikely to survive. The trust employing the consultant had to reassure the public that this would not be implemented. This supports the view that an economic measure of a human life or a person's value to society (if these can be made) are not acceptable criteria for making clinical decisions.

In practice, purchasers do sometimes refuse to authorise treatment of complex cases because of the high costs. There have been several such examples in my own hospital and other tertiary referral centres. There does not appear to be any consideration paid to the clinical aspects of the case nor to the fact that the patient may not get treatment or will have to be treated elsewhere where the outcome is likely to be less satisfactory. Of course we need to obtain data on clinical outcomes, but there is good evidence that specialised centres with a large experience of a complex condition tend to do better than general hospitals who only see the occasional case. At the moment the lack of sophistication of the audit systems and costing process means that precise information is not available. Some hospital trusts put a blanket charge on complex cases. They may profit on some, but more often lose money on such patients. As an example, if the true cost of treating a patient with severe infected pancreatitis is demanded (sometimes up to six months in hospital with many weeks in intensive care and several operations) then the purchaser is unlikely to ever allow more cases to be referred or may simply refuse to pay. The cost for such a patient can easily exceed £50,000 and about 20-30 per cent are likely to die, even in specialist centres. As trusts are now beginning to charge a daily rate for intensive therapy unit (ITU) cases, the true cost of treating such patients is now starting to emerge. There is a wide variation in the costs of ITU care between trusts but this should not enter into the formula, as the choice of centre for referral should depend only on the clinical aspects of the case. Evidence to date on referral patterns would suggest that even if local consultants were willing to transfer patients there can be opposition on the grounds of cost.

Tertiary referral centres do not always have the time to discuss the financial arrangements of a seriously ill patient and it may only become evident after treatment has been carried out that funding is not going to be made available. We have had many such cases in our hospital and our trust is then obliged to carry this cost. This resembles the situation in the USA where sometimes the uninsured may get emergency treatment at the hospital's expense. It could also lead to a backlash from specialist providers (again like hospitals in the USA or in the private sector) who will insist that financial arrangements are made before treatment is commenced. Clearly the guarantees made at the start of the NHS reforms, that complex tertiary referrals would continue to be funded, have not always been honoured.

Contract Medicine

Another effect of the NHS reforms on clinical practice is the fact that the purchasers have enormous power to reduce or curtail certain specialties. The power of the purchaser, whether in the NHS or in the private sector, is one of the new realities of medical practice.[5] The short term nature of the contracting process, which is currently on an annual basis, makes planning of hospital services very difficult. This has led to providers beginning to form consortia in order to counteract the power and demands of the purchaser.

The short term nature of the contracting process can lead to a relatively sudden withdrawal by the purchaser from a specialty. In my hospital a threat was made to stop all ENT services which had to be reversed by political pressure. Had this been implemented it would have left a large unit of four consultants, many junior doctors and other specialist staff without funding but with an ongoing demand for services from other departments such as accident and emergency (A/E) and paediatrics, quite apart from the teaching and clinical research programme which would have been left in tatters.

Hospital services may also come under threat from their own trust management, who may decide for commercial reasons to close down certain specialties which are not good money earners and concentrate resources on others. It is true that the shape of services supplied by different hospitals is the result of an evolutionary procedure and that not all specialties need exist on every site. However managers do not always realise that removing on site core services such as urology or ENT will reduce the standard of patient care in large hospitals. There is an obvious need for close cooperation amongst different specialties in the management of various clinical problems.

Another problem in London and in other major cities is over the reorganisation of specialist services. The London Implementation Group was set up to rationalise certain specialist services and this created confusion about whether trusts were operating in a market driven economy or a centrally controlled structure. This raises the interesting question as to whether or not a hospital could go against a central recommendation and develop, for example, a cardiac service in opposition to another regional centre.

The general practitioner (GP) fundholder is another unpredictable factor in the organisation of services and some see this as an advance. Certainly as a purchaser (either alone or in a consortium) the GP now has the power to influence the trusts who are obliged to scramble for patients. Many see this as a useful way to change hospital policies and improve the service. It is perhaps the nearest to a true market and most closely resembles the situation in private practice. However, there are sometimes excessive demands being made of consultants and an occasional strident threat to remove patients if these demands are not met. The ethical position is also affected by the financial aspects of fundholding. Should the GP send the patient to a hospital where the treatment is cheap or where it is clearly better but more expensive? This is a real dilemma for doctors and practice managers and it would be interesting to see if financial considerations normally prevail.

The extra-contractual referral (ECR) has become another catch phrase and management obsession. There is now less emphasis on the patient's clinical condition when prioritizing cases for treatment. Instead there is a blatant drive to 'process' the more lucrative patients and all internal hospital spread sheets are peppered with the number of ECRs and earnings thereof by different specialties. No doubt the advent of performance related pay will utilise this sort of data in setting 'bonus' pay for doctors and add to the commercial fever which is overtaking old professional attitudes.

The contracting process has also introduced a competitive element to what was previously a unified and cohesive National Health Service. Hospitals which previously co-operated with each other in a variety of ways are now in a battle for survival. Teaching hospitals may ask why they should support their competitors by rotating out high quality junior staff, when these hospitals are attempting to undercut their position in the market place by economic means. District hospitals are fearful that quality consultant staff will be lured to more successful centres and thus further undermine their own possibly precarious situation. As the market forces develop there will be inevitable winners and losers. Patients, particularly from fundholding GPs,

44

are seen as business opportunities and attempts are made by marketing departments to lure these patients from one hospital to another.

Is the Patient Better Off?

Can one argue that the patient is now getting a better deal in terms of available services? I cannot assess primary care and GP services but in London it is becoming clear that, either by rationalization or by market forces, hospital services are being curtailed. The London teaching hospitals, attacked for their élitism, their cost and in some cases their lack of a residential local community have, with some other London hospitals, borne the brunt of reorganisational changes, a situation which is extending now into other large cities. The fact that major hospitals with international reputations are being closed under the guise of rationalisation may well be perceived in the long-run as an act of wanton destruction. The argument that out of town patients can just as easily be taken care of in their local shire hospital may be true for many but not for all. We are fortunate to have had, in the UK, a high standard of consultant care throughout the country, but the need to refer on certain patients with particular conditions will remain. Moreover the presence of strong university academic departments providing active links between clinical practice and basic science was always a guarantee of high standards of research and treatment. Such units are now threatened. In some instances, as mergers take place between large hospitals, there are units being dissolved and terms such as 'asset stripping' and 'downsizing' are being employed. True, a degree of rationalisation was necessary and it was not possible for the situation in London to continue, but we are in danger of throwing out the baby with the bathwater.

The closure of hospitals and the reduction of beds in London has been an official policy for some years. This has resulted in a daily battle for entry to hospital by seriously ill patients who are hawked around from hospital to hospital. On my last emergency take a seriously injured man who had fallen out of a window and sustained multiple injuries could not be admitted because of a full ITU, and it took three hours and an approach to ten hospitals before he was shipped across London. This anecdote can be repeated over and over again and is mirrored in the A/E departments of all major hospitals as patients queue for admission, lined up on trolleys as beds are desperately sought or transfer arrangements are made.

Beds in London

The government maintains that bed numbers in London are correct but this flies in the face of day to day experience. The case against the government has been marshalled by Professor Brian Jarman. He has shown quite clearly that the number of beds per head of population in London is not satisfactory and that the figures quoted by the Department of Health which purport to show that London is overbedded are simply not true. Jarman concludes that the revenue resource allocation to London is 5 per cent *below* the expected value and this under-funding of the purchasers will have severe knock-on effects on London hospitals, even leading to 'the disintegration of health care in London'.[6] He also shows that although the acute bed provision in London is about 5 per cent above the national average, a level of 10 per cent would be appropriate given the factors leading to hospitalisation and the need to cater for non-Londoners.

The bed situation is one of the most critical problems in London. Anyone challenging Professor Jarman's figures should look at the position in the front lines and see the daily struggle for entry to hospital and the high rate of cancellation of admissions for routine surgery which now take place. This is daily proof of the fact that Professor Jarman's figures are correct. The proportion of emergency cases in my ward has risen inexorably over the last few years whilst booked elective patients are cancelled with monotonous regularity. Prior to the reforms this hardly ever occurred but now it is not uncommon for a patient awaiting surgery to be cancelled five or six times at the last minute, with serious social and psychological implications. The resulting hospital paperwork involved and the complaints procedures that so often follow make this an expensive exercise. Some surgeons in other London hospitals have long since given up any pretence of doing routine work and confine themselves only to emergencies and cases of malignancy. Patients desperate for treatment now often try to obtain care in the private sector, even if this means paying from their own pocket.

The lack of beds has led to a style of working that is both unsafe and callous. It is now quite common to send for some unprepared patient at a moment's notice to come into hospital for surgery because a bed has suddenly become free. Such a patient arriving for an operation in a state of nervous anticipation, often whilst the actual operating list is in progress, may be unseen and unprepared by the operating surgeon until he or she reaches the anaesthetic room. Whilst this may be considered an efficient use of beds and facilities, it is in fact medico-legally indefensible and is forced upon many surgeons in London by the inadequate bed base and the frenetic pace of work required to 'keep up to contract'. Some patients actually arrive in the middle of the night before major surgery, and this mad-cap pace is seen again later in the rapid and early discharge of patients from hospital resulting in greater pressure on GPs, difficulties of communication and the need for some patients to be readmitted with complications.

The mismatch between demands and funding has been recently discussed by two consultant surgeons working in Watford.[7] They point out that, although accurate information on the emergency, urgent and routine surgical caseload is not generally available in the UK, there is evidence that emergency treatment is delayed as beds are sought by GPs for sick patients, as managers may need to seek formal cover from other hospitals and as junior doctors may have to treat and transfer. They use the common clinical setting of acute appendicitis, in which it has been shown in the USA that there is higher risk of perforation in the uninsured than the insured patient due to delays in obtaining treatment. They infer that similar problems may occur in the UK. More information is needed to clarify this point but there is no doubt that delays in the NHS are an increasing problem.

Burgeoning Bureaucracy

The vast increase in managers and paperwork has come between the doctor and patient in many ways and resulted in less efficient working. Examples can be seen in the organisation of the waiting list and the booking of outpatients. Both were previously very straightforward procedures, but the need for charging has led to the introduction of gatekeepers, finance officers, marketing and clerical staff. This has resulted in delays, poor attendance by patients and fewer cases being treated on each list. Some hospitals have gone on to develop internal charging whereby users of a service must buy this from another department, i.e. a surgeon must buy his x-rays from radiology or his patients' blood tests from pathology. These types of exercise are very time consuming and illustrate how increased administration can confuse and complicate simple issues.

The advent of large hospital computer systems is at hand but so far they have not proved their worth either in terms of their programmes or in the effort required to enter the data. The fact that these work well in the private sector (albeit mainly for the financial aspects) does not necessarily mean that they will do so in the NHS where the volume of work is much higher and the quality and dedication of the relatively poorly paid clerical staff is lower. Such computers do have enormous potential for managers to analyse parameters of care such as length of stay, type of condition or operation and investigations that have been ordered and could be used to exert pressure on consultants who fail to fall into a pattern. Such a development is taking place in the private sector, with BUPA starting to send consultants their ranking in terms of length of stay for certain conditions. This is uncomfortable for the consultant who is used to clinical freedom, and clearly a line must be drawn between the professional aspects of clinical care and management interference.

The layers of administrators that have been introduced to the new health service may appear to give an indication of efficiency. From what I can gather, my own hospital is very efficiently managed by comparison with most and is balancing its books, which seems to be the prime considerations of all chief executives and trust boards. However, the general quality of managers, particularly at the middle and lower tiers, does leave much to be desired. There is no effort being made to evaluate their performance in a systematic way and a recent questionnaire study elsewhere indicated that the vast majority of managers were unsure about the way in which the hospitals were funded and were financially illiterate. At the lower levels of clerical management matters are very bad. Standards may vary around the country and generalisations must be made with caution, but in many large London hospitals the dedicated and long serving staff who used to run departments like medical records have now been supplanted by a stream of casual workers with no particular feeling of dedication to the work. There is a high rate of staff sick-leave and desperation amongst more senior managers as patient notes and X-rays are lost with monotonous regularity.

I do not believe it is helpful to divide doctors from managers as they have a mutual goal. The development of the medical and clinical director system, whereby consultants are brought into the management chain, is often said to be the bridge between the two. This may be so in some trusts but in others the medical representatives do not necessarily enjoy the confidence of the majority of their colleagues and have not been chosen by vote. Some, but by no means the majority of clinical directors, do the job for the wrong motives, and this may become exacerbated when the C merit award system involves more local management input by the chief executive or chairman of the board. A docile period as a clinical director will be seen as the required stepping stone on the merit award ladder. However there are other objections to the system of clinical directorships. There is the question of whether the director is allowed to be involved in the major strategic issues facing the trust or is merely used to execute those decisions. There is the question of whether active clinicians have the time or expertise to become involved in the *minutiae* of management and, if so, who does their clinical work and who replaces them at the end of their tenure of office, given the limited pool of consultants to draw on. Having been a director with a large budget of millions of pounds I can acknowledge the personal feeling of power that was engendered, but that was entirely illusory as the director was merely there to implement difficult organisational and financial decisions taken by others, over which he had no control.

Spread Sheet Medicine

The expansion of management has been explosive over the last few years, during which time, critics are keen to point out, there has been a contraction of nursing services. There is no doubt that, prior to the reforms, the NHS was under-managed and also that the old concept of management by a triumvirate of medical superintendent, matron and hospital governor would be inappropriate for the 1990s. The need for costing and contracting requires more management expertise, but to what degree and at what cost is unclear. It is doubtful that in the UK the situation could reach that of the USA, where 22 per cent of costs are consumed by administration, but the information on management costs is not available and can be blurred by the inclusion of secretaries and junior clerical officers in the figures. As more managers have been introduced, including doctors brought in as clinical directors, a new jargonese is employed and new committees and posts have been created (i.e. Director of Corporate Management). Spread sheet analysis is rampant and outside consultancy firms are being recruited at considerable cost to answer questions that are often self-evident and on subjects about which they often have very little expertise. Despite all this effort the clinical costing process is still in its infancy (perhaps not surprising as the task was mammoth and there was no previous yardstick) and prices vary widely between what appear to be similar institutions.

It is possible to recount a series of anecdotes about local organisational errors but this is not constructive and many could be solved by competent staff. However, from a management point of view, all may be seen as going well provided the Patients' Charter is fulfilled. This is a rather unhelpful concept and implies that hospitals and outpatients can be run like a conveyor belt factory. The publication of death rates from different hospitals will add another feature to hospital care, which would really need an expert to interpret given the complexities of case mix that go to make up the mortality figures. However there is no doubt that these simplistic figures could have a very worrying and adverse effect on patients entering hospital.

There are those who attack the medical profession for being reactionary, and no doubt the NHS reforms have moved power away from consultants in the hospital service. The allegations of those like Professor Maynard and certain trust chairmen who are virulent in their attacks on consultants do little to encourage cooperation. Another trust chairman, who wished to introduce the business ethic to the hospital service by insisting that the primary loyalty of the consultant should be to the trust organisation rather than the patient, was rapidly disowned by government ministers. However, he made a crucial point and one which is being developed by different trusts in their job plans for consultants. This is over the way in which a previously professional and public service ethos can be incorporated into a commercial style of organisation which brings with it certain obligations that are alien to a free and independent consultant body. There are wider issues affecting the independence of the medical profession which relate to the possibility that postgraduate deans could become civil servants and the Department of Health could take over the organisation of medical education.[8] If so, then the independence of the medical profession would be lost and clinical practice would be controlled by government. This would not be in the interests of the patient.

Conclusion

In summary it can be said that patients do not get a better deal following the NHS reforms, at least in London. There are many inequalities within the system and a series of problems, ranging from inadequate facilities to poor and excessive management, which make working patterns very difficult. Other changes in the pipeline, particularly those relating to medical training will also have an effect. There are some good points in the reforms, such as the power of the purchaser, in particular the GP, to influence improvements in service. However, the revolution is still in its infancy and only time will allow an answer to some of the major questions that have been posed.

Notes

1   Kaletsky, A., 'Competition Will Make Health More Expensive', *The Times*, 14 July 1994.

2   Szczepura, A., 'Finding a Way Through the Cost and Benefit Maze', *British Medical Journal*, 1994, vol., 309, p. 1314.

3   McQuay, H. and Moore, A., 'Need for Rigorous Assessment of Palliative Care', *BMJ*, 1994, vol. 309, p. 1315.

4   Feder, G., 'Clinical Guidelines in 1994', *British Medical Journal*, 1994, vol. 309, p. 1457.

5   Morrison, I. and Smith, R., 'The Future of Medicine', Editorial, *British Medical Journal*, 1994, vol. 309, p. 1099.

6   Jarman, B., 'The Crisis in London Medicine: How Many Hospital Beds Does the Capital Need?', Special University Lecture, University of London, Senate House Printing Service, 5 July 1994.

7   Thomas, J.M. and Reilly, M., Editorial, *The Lancet*, 1994, vol. 344, pp. 1381-82.

8   Browse, N., 'Independence', *Annals of the Royal College of Surgeons of England, Supplement*, 1994, vol. 76 p. 223.

Specialist Services within the Reformed National Health Service

J.I.L. Bayley

Whilst the National Health Service reforms have enhanced the abilities of specialist hospitals to develop the services which can be offered to patients, nevertheless they have also released pressures which can mitigate against such basic tenets as equality of access.

NHS trust hospital status can liberate a specialist unit to focus its efforts to improve services with much greater cohesion than could be achieved under the previous system. There is now the possibility for such units in this country to emulate the achievements of their counterparts elsewhere in the world who have clearly demonstrated their effectiveness and efficiency in delivering high class health care. Additionally the purchaser-provider split and the development of general practitioner fundholding practices (GPFH) have cut across outdated referral practices and have the potential to put patients centre stage. That they can fail to do so in individual cases, however, is due to the inequalities which have been released as a result of aspects of the reforms.

Despite the huge advances in delivery of health care which the development of the NHS has achieved, in comparison with pre-war services, there was never, of course, true equality of access. Patchy and poorly focused distribution of resources from region to region and within regions disadvantaged many; admission lists were not infrequently constructed according to the special interest of the doctor concerned; and inner city hospitals failed to deliver adequate services to their more needful local populations. The current reforms certainly afforded an opportunity to redress some of these inequities and in part they have done so, since it is very much more difficult for doctors to admit on the basis of their personal interests. However, one of the problems of the reforms is that, because this two edged weapon of clinical freedom has been severely blunted on not one but both edges, the ability of the NHS to develop and sustain specialist services has been curtailed in a number of financial and organisational ways.

There is an increased financial pressure for local consultants to treat as many conditions as possible in-house where services may be cheaper on a year by year basis but not when viewed in terms of longitudinal outcome. Unchecked, this pressure will lead to the development of services lacking in critical mass for the best outcomes and an increase in the need to manage more costly complications later; a situation exactly analogous to aspects of the American model. The trend will escalate with the ever increasing emergence of new techniques and technologies such as minimal access surgery. The reforms have failed to take these factors fully into account and will continue to neglect them until purchasing health authorities are able to take a more collective and long term view of health care delivery.

The Problem of 'Middle-Waiters'

The creation of an eighteen-month ceiling to waiting lists combined with an under-resourced service has led to discrimination against the 'middle-waiters'. In the pre-reformed health service, long waiting lists were one form of health care rationing. Although they created their own forms of inequity, the absence of an upper limit at least neutralised the financial pressures which now prevent some patients being admitted according to clinical need.

In the early phases following the reforms, it tended to be provider units which overshot their contracts and midway through the year, given the more stringent financial directives which now operate, were obliged to limit admissions to acute and urgent cases only. As providers have become more efficient at managing their contracts and as the Patients' Charter takes more effect, it is purchasing authorities who are now more likely to require providers to restrict admissions to urgent and 'long waiters' because they do not have sufficient funds for the year to cope with all cases. Thus the pressures on a surgeon arranging admissions under the influence of that directive will be to admit the long-waiter rather than a patient who might have been on the waiting list for less than a year and who cannot be counted as urgent but who, nevertheless, ought to be admitted sooner, rather than later, by virtue of increased pain or perhaps an at-risk job. The financial pressures are particularly heightened by the ruling that providers shall reimburse to the purchasing authority the cost of treating any long-waiters who have not been admitted within the stipulated time. The year-on-year increase in the country's global waiting list will further compound the problem because the great majority of those people have now been waiting less than a year and will in 1995/96 create a large bulge, tipping over into the long-wait category. Thus increasingly providers will be unable to give a timely service to the 'middle-waiters' despite, in some cases, their greater need.

Differences in performance between purchasing authorities in processing admission-approval requests can create non-clinical inequalities based on the financial imperative to control the referral process. In the 'old' NHS, patients were simply referred to wherever their clinical needs could best be met. Post-reforms, patients referred to hospitals not covered by their purchasing authority's established contracts are dealt with by extra-contractual referral (ECR) agreements. These are negotiated on a case by case basis which introduces a bureaucratic process whose main purpose is to allow the purchasing authority to keep a tight control of the ECR budget which they have earmarked for the year. Processing of ECR agreements can create particular problems for those provider units who receive patients from large areas of the country. Since patient numbers from any one purchasing authority will not be sufficiently large or frequent enough to justify creating a standing contract, these specialist services are dependent on the ECR process and need to create their own administrative departments to be able to meet the criteria laid down—strict letter-of-the-law adherence to which is required before payment will be made. Delays in gaining approval from this financially driven bureaucracy can and do lead to patients having to wait longer than they might otherwise have needed to. The tertiary referral system could deal with this issue since such referrals bring an automatic agreement to fund treatment. However this system does not function properly since, for financial reasons, there are pressures on consultants in local referring hospitals to refer patients back to their general practitioners for onward referral to the specialist centre. These patients then fall outside the net of the tertiary referral rule and agreement to treat has to be sought via the ECR route. Neither does the system take into account the need to create a health care delivery system which caters for second opinion referrals.

More Inequality

Thus the old factors contributing to inequality of access have now been added to by the effects of capping waiting times and under-assessing the effect of pressures for local health authorities to retain patients on the development of specialist services. The Department of Health's guidelines on contracting for specialist services are an ineffective counter to these pressures. If the people of this country are to realise the benefits which can clearly accrue from the NHS reforms, there is a need to recreate an ability to admit from waiting lists on the basis of real clinical priority according to laid-down parameters which can be audited from unit to unit. There is also an urgent requirement to reduce the pressures which currently exist preventing onward referral of specialist cases and which currently not only exert a downward influence on new developments but which can lock people into their locality who may be helped by new technologies and new techniques available elsewhere or who undergo inadequate surgery locally because of the financial pressures to limit outside referrals.

The Economic Fundamentals

Arthur Seldon

Abstract: *The traditional term 'patients' suggests sick people patiently awaiting or resignedly receiving treatment from medical service 'providers' paid for by a vaguely-comprehended source. The annual budget 'funding' of family doctors and local health 'authorities' as 'purchasers' with new powers to choose between alternative 'trust' hospitals, still called 'providers' but competing in terms of quality and price, begins to create an effective 'internal' market. The bargaining power of patient-customers has begun to approach that of the 'providers'. A fuller but still internal market, in which ultimately doctors would occasionally wait for patients as well as patients for doctors, would require payment directly by individual patient-customers (or for them by insurer agents). The further transition from 'internal' to 'external' markets would transform 'customers' into the 'consumers' and 'providers' into the 'suppliers' of the classical competitive market that was suppressed by government in the creation of the National Health Service. The decisive development in the future is that government may not be able to slow down the eventual transformation from the state monopoly to competing private services.*

The Economic Setting

The varied testimony assembled in this collection from family and specialist doctors in everyday contact with patients and from managers of the new institutions created since 1989 provides revealing experiences and opinions on the reforms so far. And they stimulate assessment of the conditions required for the likely and desirable developments into the 21st century.

Whatever the course of the reforms, the fundamental determinant of the quantity and quality of medical care in the NHS is the total of the resources at its command and the skills with which they are deployed. An assessment of the most favourable economic conditions for the reforms is necessary to envisage their early prospects and the further reforms that seem desirable.

Anxieties among medical professionals about the shift in decision-making from clinical to managerial authority is understandable. The question is both whether it will make better use of available resources and, moreover, in the longer run, raise new resources.

The British state medical system has been financed as in no other Western country. It has been organised within the artificial limits on supply imposed by government. The political decision in 1948 has prevented discovery of whether, and how far, patients as consumers would have preferred to allocate more of their incomes and other means to health care than the state has raised by taxes. And the politically restricted entry to the internal market has reduced the possibility of discovering the existing and potential suppliers who would make the best use of the politically restricted resources. The task now is to frame the economic principles and methods that would best discover their probable amount and deployment.

The main economic realities that will influence the working of the reforms seem to be:

1 The essential reason for the persistent inadequacy of the resources available to the NHS;

2 the financing methods required to maximise them;

3 the critical function of price (cost);

4 the conditions in which medical service is supplied: emergency, optional, incidental, cosmetic;

5 the contending influences in determining their use: clinical, judicial, individual without payment, political, economic;

6 the optimum bargaining power between 'customers' (consumers) and 'providers' (suppliers);

7 the further reforms that seem desirable to reinforce those introduced since 1990;

8 the ultimate relative strengths of politics and the market in determining the changing structure of medical care into the 21st century.

1 The Persistence of Inadequacy in Resources

Additional resources will, in almost all conceivable circumstances, produce some improvement, however slight, in medical services. This everyday sense of 'under-funding' could in time consume most of the national income. The task is rather how to decide whether or not the additional resources would do more good in medical care than in non-medical applications elsewhere.

The significant economic sense of 'under-funding' is that the state has itself limited the amount of resources. It uses only one method of financing: taxation (national insurance is a concealed form of taxation). In this form under-funding is chronic and self-inflicted by government decision.

For over 80 years British government has discouraged the use of insurance for medical care. It has raised about a fifth less resources as a proportion of national expenditure for medical care than most countries in Europe and around a half less than in North America.

This is a political limitation. The further, personal, limitation that individuals can impose is how to divide resources between medical and all other uses. In this larger setting there is no intrinsic shortage of resources for medical care. The limit is set by personal preferences for non-medical uses. The 'under-funding' of medical care in this sense is a consequence of the high standards which we all have come to expect and demand in food, clothes, homes, holidays, motoring and much else in the growing amenities of modern living.

This is the task of decision-making by individuals, entailing judgments on the sacrifices and 'opportunity costs' of the non-medical services foregone.

2 The Neglected Methods of Financing

Most people in Europe and America widely use both state and private insurance, with or without state-imposed requirements or limits. In Britain less than one in ten families adds expenditure on private insurance to its state taxation. In other countries many more families also use private insurance.

The solution for this fundamental 'under-funding' is, in principle, simply for government to allow and encourage private voluntary insurance on a much larger scale than it has been growing in recent years. The resulting increase in resources would remove much of the continuing 'under-funding' and its varied consequences—the shortages of all kinds seen in lack of beds, most lately in mixed wards without consulting the sensitivities of patients, long hours of work, relatively meagre pay and, not least, waiting by patients for consultations, examination and treatment.

Insurance financing would add the spare capacity that a buyers' market would generate. Surgeons would rarely have to search for a bed from London to Leeds, or experience long delays waiting for a bed after the decision to admit. A 70 per cent bed occupancy would not be evidence of waste but of the reserves and flexibility required in a service liable to uncertainty in the demands on its staffing, equipment and facilities.

Potential patients waiting anxiously for treatment see these shortages even more acutely than staff. The view, even among doctors, that the NHS is superior to other medical systems because it is 'cheaper' overlooks its relatively poor quality in timing. Medical care is a product or service judged supremely by its availability. That it is 'free' can mean little to the unwell and sick if it is not supplied when—and where—it is wanted. Ideally in a buyers' market there would be sufficient resources for doctors and other staff to wait for patients rather than patients for staff. In a country with the relatively high living standards of Great Britain the NHS has been backward territory.

Government health financing confined to taxes is clearly not the only way to pay for medical care. The main source of health financing in most Western countries is a combination of state insurance and private payment (by private insurance and other sources). The result is the 14 per cent of national income which is spent on health care in the USA, of which more than half is from voluntary insurance and other private sources, and the 8-10 per cent in the main countries of Western Europe. A third of the Australian 9 per cent is paid through private insurance. The UK total was around 6 per cent for many years until it rose to 7 per cent in the 1990s.

The criticism of British sociologists that the higher percentages in the USA are spent partly on 'frills' with little medical advantage commits two errors: it shows scant respect for the personal patient preferences which would be paramount if patients could pay in the ways they wished; and it mistakes the nature of modern representative government. The sick are healed in part by comforts and amenities, not least flexible family visiting when under treatment (even, research has discovered, by a favoured dog) and easy links with places of work when convalescing. And since democratic government is not an exact science, the choices are between too much expenditure on medical care and too little. Again this is a decision to be made by potential patients, not by politicians or medical suppliers. The sociologists—and medical professionals—who complain about 'under-funding' ironically often oppose the private insurance that cures it in other countries. The NHS does not consult the people on whether they prefer too little to too much; in effect it has persisted in the supposition that they prefer too little.

A possibly even larger source of financing would be to proceed from internal to external markets. Medical care competes with expenditure on all other goods and services, encouraged in other Western countries by informative and persuasive advertising. It is supplied not only in crisis but in other optional circumstances (see below).

3 The Crucial Function of Price—Individual Cost

To ensure that the poor had access to medical care the NHS removed its prices. To help the shrinking minority with low incomes it removed from all middle and higher income-groups the indispensable device the market system uses to identify the relative value of non-medical resources in alternative uses.

The removal of prices from state medical care also removes awareness of its cost. It is a basic economic law that the lower the price the higher the demand; at nil price, as in the NHS, the demand can be infinite. The instinct to think twice about whether worrying symptoms justify a visit to the doctor or a quick call at the chemist is then suppressed. The individual still pays for the state medical care, but less consciously by taxes that he cannot link to individual episodes of illness or treatment. A measure designed to help the minority poor has harmed them by making then compete with the majority non-poor for the restricted supplies made available by the state.

The poor were handicapped by another effect of the NHS. It arbitrarily enabled potential patients with family, social, or political connections or the cultural power to argue their case with medical or managerial professionals who decide access to the unpriced ('free') services. Like middle-income parents who pay the higher housing costs in areas with the better state schools, middle-income patients can often derive more from the NHS than lower-income parents by elbowing the less well-connected or cultured out of waiting lists.[1]

By restoring the buyer-seller relationship between purchasers and providers, the recent reforms begin to reintroduce the instrument of price within the NHS. But pricing could be extended more deeply and more widely.

The decisive value of the buying-selling innovation is that it provides new information in judging the relative cost of alternative services and suppliers. It restores both the 'price-effect' and the 'income-effect' of price.

In removing price from most decisions, the NHS made it difficult to assess the effect on resources available—the 'income-effect'. The 'price-effect' is even more powerful in the longer run. When buyers indicate they prefer some services or suppliers to others—by repeated orders, or by being prepared to pay higher prices for better quality (timing, place, choice of surgeon, various facilities)—the supply can be expected to increase; and the supply of other services which may be in less demand will be reduced, or possibly ended. In the 'price-less' NHS the supply-side decisions fell to be made by uninformed administrative procedures, often with a political influence far removed from the effects on the treatment and recovery of the ultimate 'customers', the sick.

The recent light thrown on decisions by new knowledge of comparative costs and prices is not generally acknowledged by medical or managerial specialists. The familiar ten-figure millions or billions used by politicians are mistaken for measures of performance. These massive macro-statistics have been made political instruments by local government officials to impress local taxpayers, but they are irrelevant in informing them of what taxpayers need to know—the individual costs of competing private services—in order to judge whether their local authorities are more efficient than private suppliers. In much the same way government health spokesmen in the Houses of Parliament use increases in macro-statistics—totals of expenditure, numbers of operations, or patients—as evidence of increased efficiency in the NHS. Taxpayers should require government to present comparative micro-statistics of the individual costs of treatments to reduce disease or save life in the NHS so that potential patients can compare and contrast them with costs in private medical services.

Within the NHS the figures required by the family doctor fundholder and health authority purchasers and by the providers are the micro-statistics of the price of each treatment or course of treatment in order to refine their buying and selling decisions.

4 From Crisis to Cosmetics

The new commercial procedures of buying and selling, bargaining and negotiating, may seem foreign to medical professionals and their clinical staffs. Some may plausibly doubt whether the time is wisely spent on assembly of information, accounting, documentation and payment and have been reluctant, despite monetary encouragement, to move from the price-less allocation system. The family practices, so far with 60 per cent of patients, and the few non-trust hospitals that remain in the allocation system are, in effect, preferring the certainties of the old-style central planning to the risks but opportunities of the new medical markets that will spread in Britain as the patient demands higher medical standards.

The doubts of the remaining price-less suppliers ('providers') and demanders ('purchasers') may partly reflect the long-standing belief, especially among the general public, that medical care is invariably delivered when patients are seriously ill and in emergency. The very word 'hospital' still conjures up impressions of crisis among the patient's family. The former workhouses reconstructed into general hospitals catered for chronic as well as acute patients (often admitted free by almoners who in effect rationed scarce but free services to the poor); they are still familiar staging posts in the folk-memory of the working classes. Hospitals as the venues of emergency and crisis are still dramatised by television series replete with screeching ambulances and blood-carrying nurses hurrying down casualty corridors.

The NHS does not supply statistics on the proportion of medical care administered in emergencies. Some medical symptoms were referred by our fathers and grandfathers to local chemists who sold homely remedies for a price: the NHS caters free for all the ailments, real or imagined, of their more affluent descendants. Yet much of medical care is optional in choice of timing to suit individual family or work commitments. Some is the outcome of known risk: on Saturday afternoons many a hospital casualty department is almost barred to the genuinely 'sick' by superficial sports injuries. And an increasing part of medical care is cosmetic.

Medical care delivery over the life-span thus varies from life-saving crisis to varying degrees of cosmetic luxury. A market of competing suppliers would be more ready than the NHS to analyse the variations in ailments and publish prices for treatments. So long as non-emergency medical care is supplied by state trust hospital 'providers' and financed by taxes, they should be required to clarify their costs to the doctor and local health authority 'purchasers'. And more widely they should account for their expenditures to the taxpayers who ultimately supply their financing. A first step is to publish their prices.

5 The Influences in Allocation

Recent cases have forced attention on the principles or influences that should govern the allocation of available resources. Five can be identified.

□ The apparently obvious principle is the primacy of alleviating pain and saving life. Clinical decisions would instinctively concentrate on these aims, whatever the costs. It has been argued above that these effects might also be obtained by changes in government financial policy and in private preferences between medical and non-medical expenditures.

Yet, whatever their good intentions, clinicians are not equipped to judge the additional benefits that a given amount of resources required to save a life would create in non-medical uses. This is perhaps the most difficult decision that falls to human beings. Yet it is made subconsciously every day by every man and woman who spends money on non-medical purchases. If the decisions by clinicians prevailed they would draw to medical care resources that might be more highly valued elsewhere. They might approach the higher percentages of national income spent on health care in other countries more quickly than other methods, but at a sacrifice of non-medical uses that taxpayers and citizens might, rightly or wrongly, prefer.

□ Judicial decision faces no less difficulty, as demonstrated by the Appeal Court judgment on the withholding by a local health authority of a bone-marrow transplant for leukaemia. It produced conflicts of opinion with superior judges in other courts, a lay health authority, the chairman of a government enquiry into medical ethics, and the Secretary of State. Compassionate judges, especially for children, would, in the prevailing state of public preferences, 'waste' resources by diverting too much into medical care.

☐ As long as the resources are limited by the state, parents *in extremis* of anxiety asking that the NHS divert resources from other uses to save the life of a child would also move 'too much' from other uses. Although the NHS has been sold for votes by one political party as 'the envy of the world' and by the other as 'safe with us', it is unable to issue to everyone blank cheques for unlimited amounts of other taxpayers' money. And it is doubtful whether politicians, even in a General Election, would venture on such extremes of political promises.

The tragedy is that if medical care were financed from a wider range of sources, including private charitable funds, voluntary insurance organisations, communal enterprises, and especially by transferring purchasing power from everyday consumer goods, such parents would be more likely to be offered gifts from strangers for medical purposes that appealed to the human heart or to pay by insurance the costs of earlier treatment.

☐ It might seem that politicians would be best equipped to decide the ideal equalisation of marginal allocations between medical and other expenditures. It could be argued that they take a wider and longer view than individuals of the eventual benefits. But these 'public benefits' are elusive measures of satisfaction to the people and they lend themselves too easily to cynical political exploitation.

Moreover suppliers of medical services who are financed by government rather than directly by patients run the opposite risk that politicians will spend *too little* on medical care. Since state medicine creates a monopoly, the bargaining power of government with both employees and fee-paid contractors enables it to depress their payments below the competitive prices that employees or contractors could expect for their services in a market in which they could move freely between competing state and private medical hospitals and other organisations. The NHS nurses who believe they are under-paid have no other ultimate recourse but to withdraw their labour by striking. And until the NHS trust hospitals become more cost-conscious and compete more among themselves and with private hospitals this is the nurses' only or main bargaining instrument.

Not least, to maintain their favour with the voting population politicians would be tempted to direct too much resources into forms of medical care, such as spectacular surgery, that earned the dramatised thanks of consumers and voters but too little into other forms, perhaps pure research, which earned fewer votes at impending elections and the eventual benefits of which might be claimed by subsequent governments of other political parties. The result of price-less monopoly medical care would be to distort the development of the most desirable medical services.

☐ The remaining principle is that of the economist: that the value of resources is maximised when no more benefit can be derived by changing from, say, state expenditure on roads to hospitals or from medical research to war widows' pensions. This position is most likely to be approached if consumers have the widest possible range of choice of expenditures between medical and non-medical service. In 1995 a switch from semi-luxury spending to private health insurance seems likely to avoid long waiting for hospital treatment. The numbers recruited by Norwich Union and other new insurers indicate a fundamental long-term trend.

6 The Bargaining Power of Buyers and Sellers

The reforms have changed the market relationships of buyers and sellers.

The purchasers—fund-holding family doctors and local health authorities—now overtly appear what they were always supposed to be: agents of the ultimate consumer, the individual citizen and taxpayer as potential patient. But the market relationships have been changed.

The NHS in 1948 revolutionised the relationship between the bargaining power of the buyers and sellers of medical care: it changed the buyers' market into a sellers' market. The new reforms now restore the element of a buyers' market, with a difference.

The fundamental difference is the market power in the relationship between buyer and seller. The pre-NHS buyers' market had emerged spontaneously in the late 19th century market. In a buyers' market the customers who pay have the edge over the suppliers who are paid; competing sellers have incentives to give of their best to their customers. In a sellers' market the suppliers who are paid have the edge over the buyers who pay: sellers lack the same immediate incentive.

The historic change to the NHS in 1948 was presaged by the doctor who said in 1910 in the *British Medical Journal* that the new government health insurance scheme would enable doctors 'to give our services to the buyer', whom he saw as 'not the poverty-stricken wage-earner but the solvent State Insurance Company'.[2] The scheme was introduced in 1911, when the Liberal Government required 12 million employees to subscribe to national health insurance. By then some nine million had been subscribing for several decades spontaneously to voluntary, private, competing Friendly Societies and medical associations of several kinds.[3]

Unfortunately the doctors of the time put their money on the wrong horse. The National Insurance system became in effect a fraud which maintained not a National Insurance Fund but a leaky tank that in recent decades paid out in cash benefits the national insurance contributions almost as soon as they were received, so that in time no fund was accumulated. And the 'poverty-stricken wage-earner' has advanced increasingly to the standing of middle-income earner who has come to expect rising standards not only in personal and household services but also in medical care.

7 Further Early Reforms

The reforms since 1989 could be reinforced by several to strengthen their market-creating effects. The general purpose and the eventual aim is both to strengthen competition among suppliers and to provide purchasing powers for individuals with incomes too low to pay the market costs of medical care. Four short- or longer-term measures suggest themselves out of many that government should now be considering urgently:

☐ the pricing of all medical treatments, with payment excused solely on criteria of income rather than other conditions, such as age, which is not necessarily related to income;

☐ encouragement—by tax concessions, removal of legal restrictions and other measures—for personal insurance with competing private organisations from Friendly Societies and similar self-help organisations to commercial insurers;

☐ the gradual privatisation of all hospitals to put the patient first by minimising the bureaucracies, avoiding waste, reducing obstruction to further reforms from the medical professionals and the employees' trade unions;

☐ many people are surviving much longer than envisaged when the NHS, free for all for all time, was created in 1948; some will want to provide comfort for their final years, perhaps with medical care in nursing homes beyond the means of the tax-financed NHS; British government of all parties could take a leaf from the Republican Party's Contract with America by providing tax concessions for private long-term care insurance.

8 The Relative Influences of Politics and the Market

Too much attention in the discussions of health policy has been paid to the activities of politicians, too little to the power of ordinary people in a market, the customers/consumers, or potential patients.

For the mass of the people shopping is more effective than voting. This is true of medical care as for other consumer goods and services. First, their real incomes are rising and they will become impatient with weeks of waiting for consultations, months for examinations, and years for treatments. The time of potential patients can be more valuable than the time of some doctors. Second, accelerating innovation in medical science and servicing, such as day surgery in which Britain is behind other countries, is creating new treatments for which more people down the income scale will be able and anxious to pay.

These changes in both the demand for and the supply of better medical care will fundamentally affect the structure of the medical care industry. The most realistic response from government is to accept not only that it no longer has a monopoly in medical care; it must also accept that it can no longer control the rate at which ordinary people will want to pay for private medicine that is more responsive to their wishes and requirements.

If the reforms are not deepened and widened to accept the accelerating changes in internal and external economic conditions, the medical and non-medical providers (suppliers) who do not embrace the reforms promptly, and indeed obstruct further reforms, will lose their purchasers, who are the ultimate customers/consumers, sooner than they would wish.

Notes

1 The evidence is assembled in Le Grand, J., *The Strategy of Equality*, Allen & Unwin, 1982.

2 *British Medical Journal*, 12 November 1910, p. 1556.

3 The history is graphically portrayed by Green, D.G. in *Working-Class Patients and the Medical Establishment*, Aldershot: Temple Smith/Gower, 1985; and re-examined for remedies by Yarrow, G. and Beenstock, M., in 'Welfare: the Lost Century', *Economic Affairs*, London: Institute of Economic Affairs, October, 1994.

The Democratic Solution

Peter Collison

A Passionate Debate

'They are going to bulldoze the Cenotaph.'

'Go on!'

'They are. It will ease the traffic flow down Whitehall'.

Of course the whole nation would have exploded at such a proposal. First in disbelieving laughter. And then in angry exasperation.

Mrs Bottomley's proposal to close or merge Barts and other great medical centres in London was not of this order but it was received in something of the same fashion. Sir Bernard Tomlinson, the gentle and distinguished pathologist and medical administrator who had had a large hand in fashioning the proposals, found himself harangued in the street by total strangers indignant at what he was suggesting. A well known consultant published a letter in *The Times* expressing blank incredulity that an institution that was already old in the service of patients before Magna Carta was signed could now be contemplated for closure.

It is worth noting this storm that burst about Mrs Bottomley because comparable storms can and frequently do occur wherever closures, mergers or almost any sort of change in health provision is attempted. Although, outside London, they may not attract national publicity, they are no less real and together serve to illustrate the fact that the National Health Service and its centres of operation occupy a unique place in the national consciousness. There is a great and dense complex of attitudes and emotions surrounding and penetrating the service in all its aspects. In some ways it has the characteristics of a mystical church in which awe, faith, and worship are more in evidence than rational calculation, function, and mundane everyday work. Sir James Gorst, one of Mrs Bottomley's more effective critics, understood this when he made the main thrust of his attack not the substance of her proposals but the style and lack of sensitivity which characterised their presentation.

The neo-Cartesians and the votaries of the dismal science who are now coming to occupy a new and significant role in the health scene would do well to appreciate this special place the service occupies and to modify their approach accordingly. This does not mean that a rational reordering of present provision is impossible nor that concessions have to be made to obscurantism. Look to South Tyneside, for example. There the Ingham Infirmary is woven deep into the life of the community and has been a locus in which for generations many personal joys and tragedies have been experienced. Its name rings along the Tyne from Gateshead to the sea with as deep a resonance as the names Barts and St Thomas' ring along the Thames. The Ingham was recently closed and now appears as a new wing to the General Hospital in South Shields. Opposition to this change was countered by gentle, patient, and thorough argument and presentation. So it *can* be done. But only if we recognise the special nature of the health service and the extra effort of understanding, argument and presentation that this requires.

There are many reasons why health services arouse deep passion and occupy a particular place in the national psyche. We here mention only one—doctors.

Doctors are an élite. They have a special relationship with their patients and with the communities in which they work. They are highly selected and represent some of the best people in each generation. They undergo a long and demanding training and at the end of it are tempered by punishing work schedules which compare with the fearsome initiation trials imposed on young warriors in some primitive societies. Not surprisingly all the numerous sociological studies of occupational prestige show doctors to be at the apex of society's status pyramid.

Recent reforms in the health service have impinged heavily on this élite and the success of the reforms clearly depends to a large extent on its support. The papers assembled here reflect the opinions, the experience, the assumptions, the sensitivities and cast of mind of this élite. The process of argument and persuasion that we have asserted to be particularly necessary in this field can well begin here.

Under-funding—Again

There is a concern over funding. Glazer begins and Laing ends with a complaint of under-funding. Of course they are absolutely right.

I have never yet been in any health premises and failed to notice or had drawn to my attention some way in which more money could be spent to advantage. But there are insistent demands for more public expenditure on nursery education, research, social services, overseas aid—the list is endless. And the unfortunate politician is pressed from the other side by the glum and obdurate tax payer. Perhaps a new government would spend more on health. But even if it did it is certain that it would not spend enough. The cry of under-funding would remain with us and might even increase, because the demand for health provision seems to grow faster than the supply. I am also a little wary of claims of 'under-funding' because they can be a diversion from problems meriting immediate attention. Once, when visiting health premises, I was impressed and abashed when met by a vigorous and convincing demand for more resources. Shortly afterwards it transpired that this particular area was making rather poor use of the resources it already had. Of course the health lobby will have to go on complaining of under-funding simply to keep its place against other interests. I am in no position to complain as I have on occasion joined in the chorus as loudly as anyone. But so far as serious discussion is concerned perhaps we could recognise that the general demand for more funding is both a platitude and a nonsense. Perhaps it could be set to verse which we could then chant at health meetings rather like a grace before serious proceedings begin.

A Golden Age?

> The experienced nurse who knew the patients, their clinical and other problems and who was trained and prepared to deal with their wound dressings, injections intimate examinations and so forth is being supplanted by a transient, untrained individual with no experience. (p. 36)

Really? Everyone has to be allowed a little hyperbole of course, and the past is another country, often seen in a rosy haze of nostalgia. The danger is that present difficulties in the health service will be seen in an exaggerated way by contrast with an idealised pre-reform past.

Now (sic) that money is part of the equation... (p. 17)

Money always was, of course, but in a particular way that made it virtually invisible in many situations. We had what was really a rather comfortable scheme of rationing. Urgent cases were seen quickly and the remainder were placed in a queue. Patients dissatisfied with queuing could pay and have themselves effectively redefined as 'urgent'. This was a useful safety valve, although there was some feeling that it bore inequitably on the poor. However, no one was explicitly denied treatment on grounds of cost. Doctors had the feeling that their decisions were purely clinical, uncorrupted by considerations of cost. Perhaps they couldn't feel otherwise except in a very general way, because detailed data on costs and resource utilisation did not start to be produced until the middle and late 1980s.

I sometimes wonder if decisions were so purely 'clinical' in the golden pre-reform years as is now often supposed. I recall many years ago a consultant friend, newly appointed, keen and possibly somewhat naïve. Having prescribed a series of treatments for a patient with, admittedly, a poor prognosis, he found the treatments subsequently discontinued because they were too expensive in terms of nurses' time. It was pointed out to him that, if he made a fuss, it could result in nurse cover being withdrawn from some of his other beds.

The division between resource/effort on one side and prognosis/clinical judgment on the other is a shadowy one. In practice there must always have been many overlapping decisions even though they were formally defined, and even felt subjectively by those taking them, to be purely clinical.

However this may be, there is certainly a problem with the new system. The problem is not, I think, that economic considerations have been brought into the health field from which previously they were absent. It is rather that many of the 'understandings', compromises, fudges and illusions of the old system are being blown away and the system is coming to be seen in the cold light of the more precise and rational terms implied in the word 'equation'. The new spirit sits ill with the traditions of health service provision and the complex of attitudes and emotions which surround it. Not surprisingly there are growing tensions. Some of these tensions may be no more than the friction that accompanies any process of change and which will moderate and then disappear as the new system matures. The present difficulties between fundholding GPs and the remainder may well be of this order. Others are more serious and, unless attended to, will fester.

Doctors vs Managers

One such, which is probably the most important, is the growing tension between doctors, particularly consultants, and the emerging class of managers. Each represents a different type of what sociologists call 'authority'. They are inevitably in opposition to some extent and, as the authority of one increases, so that of the other has to diminish. The architects of the new system must have had this in mind when they created clinical directorates. This was obviously a way of binding professionals into the system and, by creating a role in which both types of authority could be mixed, of giving decisions which are, in part or in whole, managerial in character, a patina, at least, of professional authority.

I think the creation of this new role is sensible and will do something to persuade doctors principally, but other professionals too, to work fruitfully with the new system to the general benefit. But there is plenty of evidence in this collection that tensions still exist and are growing. There is the fear that the new clinical directors will be simply poachers turned gamekeepers, used to impose decisions in which they have no great part in fashioning. Some managers are said to be attacking problems with 'relish' (p. 36) if the proposed solution is likely to be less than palatable to the professional side. The general quality of managers leaves 'much to be desired' (p. 47). The attacks on consultants from some quarters are 'virulent' (p. 49) and there are features of practice 'not apparent to non-clinical managers' (p. 36).

The tensions between the two sides are more and more likely to cause splits which are occasionally going to burst into public view. One such split which has recently attracted publicity in the Northern Region illustrates the problem.

In one part of the Region a directive has been issued limiting treatment for infertility to women under a certain age. A consultant made it known that he had received this directive and felt obliged to abide by it. A spokesman for management demurred at the words 'directive' and 'rationing' and suggested that 'guidelines' expressed the situation more accurately. 'Guidelines' is a nice word, redolent of the conventions that governed the old system. But the director of a clinic, commendably enthusiastic for the service, roundly declared that treatments withheld on grounds of cost would be declared to be so. No fudging here, therefore, of the line between clinical and economic. Warmth has been added to the situation by the appearance of a vigorous public pressure group demanding recognition of the problem of infertility, which it claims is widespread, and increased provision for its treatment. Additional exasperation has been caused because some areas imposing limits by age have chosen different ages from others as the ceiling.

At one time situations such as this could have been managed privately and within the conventions of the system. Now they appear as a clear conflict between the two types of authority—management and profession. And this Northern dispute, made public and explicit in its detail, touches dimensions which transcend both those of management and clinical decision. One body of opinion, for example, is opposed to infertility treatment, in some of its forms at any rate, on the basis of moral or religious convictions. Others give it a low priority for treatment—higher than, say, the removal of tattoos, but lower than some other demands—and in justification of their position they point to the opportunity to adopt or foster for those who have a strong and unfulfilled desire to nurture. The pressure group, on the other hand, regards infertility as a medical condition, somewhat akin, perhaps, to a broken leg and meriting urgent treatment at the public expense. There is the additional problem of likely outcomes. Should patients with a low chance of success be treated on the same terms as others with a better chance? And what chances of success should be required? Five per cent, twenty per cent? Should there be an age limit? If so, where should it be set?

Stated in this bald way it is obvious that there is no definitive answer to these questions either in clinical or management terms. Similar questions lie behind many of the experiences and observations related in this collection. We have suggested that many health policy questions in the past have been not exactly resolved but rather dissolved away in a consensus which was acceptable, partly because of the opaque nature of the system, and partly because of the special place that doctors in particular, and the health service generally, occupy in society. The recent reforms have disturbed the old consensus. Questions that previously might have been fudged and dissolved away are now pressed forward for conscious and calculated resolution. A complicating feature is that patients, with much official encouragement, are no longer the docile recipients of 'doctor knows best' but are more sophisticated and demanding.

There are many problems in the public arena which contain elements incommensurate one with another and which cannot be solved by reference to any one element alone. We deal with them by public discussion and voting. This collection persuades me that we need urgently to look at the governance of the health service to see how it might be reshaped to provide opportunities for this sort of solution.

The Political Dimensions

Present structures are certainly ill-suited. Trusts, for example, are controlled by chairmen and directors who are appointed through a political/administrative process, and by senior members of staff. Chairmen and directors have been chosen principally for their experience of management. This has certainly been an asset to trusts in their first stages. But appointees have no popular mandate and they are exposed to the charge of being placemen of the political party in power. This is unfair but the charge has been pressed effectively in the party political arena and has reduced the acceptability and authority of health decisions. Of course the service in all its particulars is ultimately responsible to the Secretary of State and through her to Parliament. But this presents only a distant prospect and it is unrealistic to expect all the numerous and variegated questions arising in the service to be aired and settled on this level.

At local level there are Community Health Councils, but they too have no popular mandate, they are poorly resourced and are largely ineffectual in policy matters. There are patient surveys, complaints procedures and vigorous departments of public relations which help providers to communicate with their populations. These were all useful lubricants which smoothed the working of the old consensus but they are no substitute for reform of the structure.

The form that a new structure might take obviously needs careful and detailed consideration, but as a first shot in this direction I suggest we might think of elected Health Boards. Obvious parallels would be with local councils elected by, and responsible to, local residents; or, perhaps, companies with boards responsible to shareholders. Senior members of health staffs could serve and advise Boards, much as senior officials serve local councils now. Some might be coopted to the Board. Care would have to be given to the definition of electorates. Limits might have to be placed on the voting rights of members of health staffs and on their rights to stand as candidates for membership of Boards which employed them. There are clearly many other details which would have to be worked out.

An alternative would be simply to make health a branch of local government, dealt with much as social services, for example, is now. Although this in many ways is a logical and attractive solution it is probably not feasible for political reasons.

The Democratic Solution

A democratically elected Board could be expected to bring all the advantages that normally come with this form. A public dissatisfied with the conduct of its Board could vote it out of office. Board members would have to face their electorates and account for themselves. Subject to the discipline of the ballot box, they would have to be sensitive to public opinion. Pressure groups and particular interests would be able to campaign, put up candidates, lobby Board members and generally would have an opportunity to influence the shape of budgets and the direction of policy.

The two types of authority, professional and managerial, which we have suggested are increasingly in opposition, as well as other parts of the service which are in conflict, would be subject to an overriding authority—that of public opinion. Clinicians, for example, finding a particular service limited by other than clinical concerns, would know that the restrictions on them came from a balance struck between a variety of interests and considerations and that the balance had on it the *imprimatur* of a democratically expressed public opinion. For their part, managers and patients too could take comfort in this knowledge. If it gave them less comfort than they felt entitled to, they could use the democratic process to try to change matters.

All this is, of course, no more than a civics-lesson recital of the advantages of democracy—a lesson we have yet to learn in health provision. Considering the experiences here related of doctors in our health service, I am persuaded that it is time we learnt the lesson and gave democracy a chance.

Giving the Reforms a Chance

Sir Richard Storey

My appointment as a non-executive trust chairman to the NHS in 1991 was effectively made locally, being recommended to the Secretary of State by the then regional chairman, who found my biography in the local newspaper directory and thought my experience suitable! This experience includes a university education, a commission in the RNVR, seven years spent practising as a barrister, and 25 years in industry. The £20,000 a year I get, as a contribution towards the fees I could otherwise earn in the time I spend on this job, is not the reason I do it: I took it simply because I was asked to serve.

York is what is known as a National Health Service whole district trust which means it serves everybody from acute operations to physiotherapy at home. Its annual turnover is £90 million and its capital expenditure £10 million: this puts it in the top 10 per cent of the 433 trusts. 80 per cent of its 250,000 local population is served by some 35 GP fundholders. It provides services to GPs and patients beyond this area across 600 square miles. Since it was started in the second wave in April 1992 it has recruited 12 new consultants (plus 17 per cent) to broaden and add excellence to its services, some of which it is developing.

The Board has five executive directors, each of whom is at the top of their profession and, including myself, six non-executives who bring wide experience from industry, previous health authority work, university health economics, and the consumer market place.

Old health authority managers and some journalists think that anyone working in private enterprise hangs up his ethics and his morality on the umbrella stand before he goes to the office. I find, on the contrary, that most people working in the private sector take their standards with them, and certainly my business experience has been dominated by the belief and expectation that ethical standards can guide business every bit as much as they can guide private life. There is no reason to suppose that the health service has been tainted by any amoral private sector managers but, conversely, some reason to believe that some NHS standards may actually have been improved by the presence of private sector executives!

I immediately noticed the immense dedication of almost all the employees who brought to their work a commitment similar to that I have found among the very best of those who work in a family-controlled business, but without any of the hostility occasionally generated in such a business by those who took their lead not from the board of directors but from the head offices of trade unions. The dedicated involvement of health service staff who serve their patients with focused motivation is most impressive. Those who work in industry must apportion their duty between their consumers, fellow employees, and shareholders (in that order). In the health service the 'shareholder' (government representing tax payers) is generally ignored! It used to be just assumed that government would provide inexhaustible money.

In practice this Government's or any government's money is bound to be finite and inadequate, given that medical science is far outstripping any government's ability to tax its subjects to provide all the help that all the people would like at the time that they would like it.

Fundamentally, I saw my job on a new trust board as influencing the use of resources to their optimum. This also involves persuading the conveyor of those resources (the purchasers and GP fundholders) to give more to York Trust if it could demonstrate that it could use those resources better than other trusts. The competitive spirit is thus now harnessed, as it is in industry, for the health service.

The Pursuit of Excellence

The pursuit of excellence was already inherent in the NHS: it was the means of achieving it that was often lacking.

Whilst I found that many in the health service were a long way behind private industry in using the tools of trade, their spirit of adventure was as good as any. They all pulled in the same direction, whereas in industry the trade unions, for many years, pulled in the wrong one—the general secretaries often fighting for more badly paid jobs rather than fewer well paid ones.

I was struck by the many NHS employees who hungered for the tools that would permit them to realise their ambitions, although it must be admitted that the occasional consultant could exhibit the 1960s thinking of the print unions! My personal GP is fond of telling me that 'doctors are worse than the dockers', and while perhaps a small number are, one should not overlook the difficulty they have had in coming to terms with the fact that, though their training had turned out brilliant consultants, their experience of modern management styles and methods was, inevitably, slight.

Patient or Customer?

Whilst the personal good intentions of senior health service personnel might be impeccable, their utilisation of resources was often poor. Of the many stories I was to hear, one of a consultant was most revealing. He was challenged by a patient who wrote: 'As a customer, I think you have treated me badly; I protest ...' The consultant replied, 'Had I realised you were coming to me as a customer, not as a patient, I wouldn't have treated you in the first place'. The concept was that the patient should be servile whereas industry's concept of the last 20 years has been that the customer is king. I understand that the British Medical Association has opposed every reform this century: no one should, therefore, be too surprised or too concerned that some doctors still oppose the recent ones. An example of this reaction was the early response in 1994 by the Royal College of Surgeons to those trust managers who asserted their right to assess the quality of the new endoscopic services being provided by surgeons. The Royal College told one trust management to mind its own business! It was not long afterwards that the College itself, after a number of complaints across the country, introduced the very standards that that trust management had previously been seeking and had, by then, already installed.

Many criticisms of trusts are directed at the *minutiae* by those who don't want to or cannot distinguish the wood from the trees. No organisation is perfect throughout, and to judge the excellence of any organisation by reference only to details is absurd. Thus, the person who criticises the whole of the National Health Service by reference to the unfortunate incident allegedly concerning a needle left in a baby, out of the many millions of daily acts of care, is like criticising the whole of the work of

Cézanne by reference to one ugly flower in one picture. Even if the critic were to find 10 poor Cézannes, it would still not behove him to say Cézanne was a bad artist. And yet the critics take specific incidents from the entire health service from which to portray it in a bad light, whereas there is substantial evidence to show that it is becoming an increasingly excellent service with an increasingly large number of very well satisfied users.

It was not only staff representative bodies which felt threatened by the reforms. The National Association of Health Authorities (NAHA, the employers' organisation representing the National Health Authorities pre-reforms) smartly added to its name a T, for Trusts, to make NAHAT, seeking to secure its own future without, in my opinion, paying proper heed to the true requirements of its members. Fortunately, now, the recently re-invigorated Trust Federation exists specifically to help trusts better to serve their public. Such a federation, working exclusively for all trust providers of services, is vital as all relevant experience of employer associations clearly demonstrates that only a closely focused association, such as is the Federation, concentrating solely on its own members' needs, is able to serve such members effectively. For NAHAT to seek to offer a bifurcated service to provider trusts as well as to purchaser health authorities when the essential interests of these two must often, and expressly by the design of the reforms, be diametrically at variance, is at best naïve and at worst mischievously subversive of the Federation's efforts. It should be obvious to everyone that frequently, such as for example in all the areas surrounding the philosophies of contract negotiations between the purchasers and providers, one organisation cannot possibly advise both camps. In industrial terms that would like an association of raw material suppliers seeking to amalgamate with the manufacturers' association representing the users of those raw materials!

There has been plenty of scope for self-indulged self-interest to scorn the reforms, as Sir Maurice Shock, former Rector of Lincoln College, Oxford, noticed when he opened a meeting to discuss the core values of medicine in November 1994 and told the doctors' representatives:

> Doctors seem to imagine that they are living in Gladstone's world of minimal government, benign self-regulation, and a self-effacing state.

In fact, instead of the rights of man we have the rights of the consumer, the social contract has given way to the sales contract, and, above all, the electorate has been fed with political promises ... about rising standards of living and levels of public service.... The appearance of the consumer society together with medical advances on an unprecedented scale and the rise and rise of the geriatrics has meant that the doctor is different, the patient is different, and the medicine is different. In short, everything is different except the way you organise yourselves.

Consultants Scrutinised

Sometimes those opposing the reforms are consultants who have found their routines challenged and, worse still, their activities monitored for managerial purposes! The public is shocked to find that a consultant, like every other person in the world, is human and can act imperfectly. There are bad barristers, company directors, architects, and doctors. Whilst management never expects, save quite exceptionally, to detect a poor consultant, inevitably it has to be management's duty to monitor the performance of all employees. And thus the anonymous consultant who allegedly used to enter the operating theatre demanding a pair of scissors with which to cut off the tabs of his operating gown that then fell to the floor for the sister to collect and take to the sewing room, had to be persuaded to change a habit—as would any consultant whose operating skills appeared to be below standard or who worked outside his contractual terms. While I welcome government league tables as helping to raise standards, what management regards as the necessary steps to raise standards even higher, others can feel is simply managerial interference. Whereas in other western countries reasonable expenditure on management is generally applauded, because it leads directly to increases in efficiency, in this country those who oppose the reforms tend to decry management expenditure as *prima facie* wasteful.

Particular criticisms of the reforms come from Londoners, but the whole country must not be judged by the idiosyncrasies of the London teaching hospitals, at least some of whose troubles have been brought upon themselves by their refusal to move, unlike St George's (ex-Hyde Park corner) which, when the moment was right, went to Tooting, where it has flourished ever since.

Undoubtedly Government's imposition of the Patients' Charter will cause some problems, for example where those who have been waiting a long time for an operation on a less serious ailment may be treated before those who have been waiting a shorter time for a more important one. Although somewhat politically inspired, there is no doubt that Government's waiting list initiatives are applauded by the public and are impossible to resist. One result should be that relatively trivial conditions never reach the waiting list. Of course if ever enough money were available for even the more trivial conditions to be done quickly, that would be Utopia. Again, we shouldn't let these relatively detailed matters in the short term distort our judgment of the change in the whole over a longer period.

While some consultants may still resent what they see as management interference with their work and procedures, many more cooperate closely with management in setting up clinical directorates and clinical boards where management and consultants work closely together with the one aim of bringing optimum care to the optimum number of people. Before 1990 the incentive for doctors and managers to collaborate on such boards was weak. Of all the changes, this style of collaborative co-operation is the most likely to bring immense benefits as the best managerial strategies and tactics encourage the best consultant practices to improve and to develop even better services for the future. Whilst consultants are well able to manage the kinds of activities that are now shown to be essential in the health service, it goes without writing that management cannot produce the health treatment without the most able consultants. Bringing together those able consultants with able management is undoubtedly a major potential triumph of the reforms. That triumph is available wherever men and women of goodwill are prepared to pool their talents.

Much management expertise brought to the health service by the reforms has been immensely valuable and is now beginning to show important improvements in health care. This will always mean monitoring by management and, in the continuing debate, perhaps one should not forget that all shop stewards dislike monitoring by management and regard it as interference!

There is a number of specific areas where the introduction of modern business practices by those recruited from industry to trust boards have brought benefits.

Financial Reporting

Before the reforms, capital arrived like manna from heaven and the hungry NHS gobbled it, barely bothering to drop on its collective knees to pray for more. Now there is a standard of financial reporting of such elegance and effectiveness that trust board members can make decisions based upon it.

More specifically, before such capital expenditure is approved, there now has to be a full and proper justification for its real cost. Previously capital could be spent with little comparison or competition between different demands for it, without much specifically costed understanding of the benefits it would bring, with little precise measurement of such benefits that it did bring, and without any concern for the actual costs of capital!

For many years much private industry has had audit committees and remuneration committees. The reforms introduced these to the NHS.

Information Technology

The lack of information generally has been the Beecher's Brook of many a hospital in the past. Whilst I cannot claim that every trust has met these challenges to its entire satisfaction, some have made excellent progress. In York, we have recently installed a new workforce system which is designed to integrate in one place all the information about our employees and support the range of employment processes from paying staff, through recruitment, training, and absence monitoring to human resource planning. With this system I know that our sick-leave rate of 3.8 per cent compares well with industry generally. We now know far more about all procedures and activities than ever before. All the forward looking staff, (which is to say most of them) welcome this progress and are very keen to use the new I.T. techniques to improve their operating performances and their administrative systems.

Employment Policy

This was simply out of date. There was little, if any, job evaluation, salary structure, job structure, briefing, local pay negotiation, local contract negotiation, and few attempts to introduce these had been made. Even now there is a long way to go before this is satisfactory. Management has little discretion to obtain an audit of a consultant's work without the latter's agreement, and some may resent the intrusion into what they still feel is their sole responsibility. In industry, if an employee appears to be under-performing, management would automatically call for an appropriate investigation. In the health service, while one may investigate the doubtful performance of a nurse, management still cannot, in many circumstances and as of right, investigate a consultant. However, often directly as a result of pressures from purchasers/users of the services, hospital trusts are now seeking sensitive and suitably confidential means whereby a consultant whose work has been questioned in the market place should have that work audited and approved or disapproved. All consultants are actually paid the same basic salary regardless of the work they do, the demand for their expertise, or any other of the criteria that generally determine salaries in other professions. NHS 'merit awards', paid on top of basic salary, are set with little involvement of managers in the hospital that employs the consultants so rewarded.

Many will hope that the spirit of the reforms does not cease to enliven Whitehall and that areas presently largely outside trust control (e.g. consultants' merit awards and truly local pay bargaining) are brought within it as Government becomes more confident that its wards can be trusted to behave properly with the grown-up toys with which they have been entrusted. Some trusts are imaginatively cooperating with private medicine so as to bring in more money with which to provide more resources for public patients.

Customer Care

An intense desire to care for patients inspired health service employees, but their ability to serve patients as customers was absent. In our first annual report I wrote that '... we probably have taken more soundings from the public over the last 12 months than in the previous 12 years!' This was arguably the most fundamental change of any because it went to the root of all activities. Everything we now do is geared to serving not a docile patient but the increasingly demanding customer. As I write this, we have experts examining with us what truly is the expectation of the patient. Everybody knows what they think it is, but few seem to have professionally analysed patient demand and then worked to meet it.

General Efficiency and Effectiveness

There have been major quests for and achievements in providing new styles of treatment. For example, we opened our Day Unit in April 1993 and are now treating patients at the rate of 14,000 per year. Many, especially the younger and more progressive consultants, warmly welcomed the Day Unit; it was also hugely popular with the public. A few consultants, initially, may have washed their hands of it—asserting that their procedures were not suitable for day treatments. Most now strongly welcome its use and, of course, from the hospital point of view, day treatment is excellent—saving the hospital the 'hotel' costs of laundry and overnight stays so that such money can be spent on treatments. From the patients' point of view, they can book in more easily, their surgery is less intrusive, their recuperation period shorter, and their day stay means a much easier home routine. There were those who protested that such practices were impossible and undesirable, especially as too many people would be sent home too soon. In fact almost all have been treated admirably and discharged appropriately.

York's Chief Executive tells me that the doubling in the rate of day surgery over two years could never have been achieved under the old order: innovations of established best practice could take a leisurely decade or two. Sub-standard services that GPs had grumbled about impotently for years and years have suddenly been sorted out because these same GPs now hold the purchasing power.

In passing, I must observe that it never ceases to amaze me that the thousands of letters of appreciation that arrive every week to the trusts are largely ignored by the media, while the relatively few mistakes reach the headlines. Recently a correspondent to our local newspaper opened his letter with the words: 'As it is almost impossible to pick up a paper or listen to a news programme without reading or hearing some criticism of the National Health Service, I thought I would like to show you there is another side to the coin. Some three weeks ago I had the misfortune of a heart attack, a very traumatic experience, but from the time the 999 call was made I have nothing but praise for the subsequent action'. It is that correspondent's experience that is typical, but a visitor from outer space reading or listening to the nation's views would suppose entry to an NHS establishment was close to receiving a death sentence!

Market Disciplines

Yet another example of trusts now being increasingly market-led to the benefit of users is the determination to test the market for many of the services that previously were just assumed must be 'in-house'. Whilst it may be easy to test the cost of, say, catering, it may be less easy to test the cost of medical services. Whilst some areas may resist market-testing, well organised managements will ensure that no services suitable for market-testing, whether medical, laundry, waste disposal or others may be allowed assume a God-given right to remain unchallenged in their cosy customs. If the trusts do not do it then health authorities and GPs will subject even medical teams to market-testing. This is but one more desirable product of the reforms.

There still remains plenty of scope for further implementation of market disciplines. Why, for example, should there be several hospitals within, say, 50 miles of one another but all with separate administrative staff? Why are so few capitally expensive machines used around the clock? Why are so few expensive premises used in the evenings and at weekends?

Accountability

In the old world there were no annual reports and accounts. There was little attempt to promote services. Now many trusts have first-rate reports and accounts widely distributed to staff, health purchasers, local authorities, and the public generally. Many have house magazines and newsletters sent throughout their catchment areas to potential patients. Great efforts have been made to ensure that the public knows what is available and can demand an explanation if it is not. Writing an annual report and account is not easy and is another area where expertise from the private sector has been invaluable. In many such ways trusts make themselves available to greater public scrutiny as opposed to the charades of yesterday's public board meetings. In York we have three public meetings a year when any question can be raised. We make available to the staff and the public the minutes of all our Board meetings.

Contracting

Nearly all the trusts in the country are having to sign annual contracts for all the services they provide in March each year, which makes contracting a mechanical process, stifling rather